INTRODUCING ISSUES WITH OPPOSING VIEWPOINTS®

Autism

Lauri S. Scherer, *Book Editor*

GREENHAVEN PRESS

A part of Gale, Cengage Learning

Detroit • New York • San Francisco • New Haven, Conn • Waterville, Maine • London

GALE
CENGAGE Learning·

Elizabeth Des Chenes, *Director, Content Strategy*
Cynthia Sanner, *Publisher*
Douglas Dentino, *Manager, New Product*

For more information, contact:
Greenhaven Press
27500 Drake Rd.
Farmington Hills, MI 48331-3535
Or you can visit our Internet site at gale.cengage.com

For product information and technology assistance, contact us at

Gale Customer Support, 1-800-877-4253
For permission to use material from this text or product, submit all requests online at www.cengage.com/permissions

Further permissions questions can be e-mailed to permissionrequest@cengage.com

Articles in Greenhaven Press anthologies are often edited for length to meet page requirements. In addition, original titles of these works are changed to clearly present the main thesis and to explicitly indicate the author's opinion. Every effort is made to ensure that Greenhaven Press accurately reflects the original intent of the authors. Every effort has been made to trace the owners of copyrighted material.

Cover image copyright © ZouZou/Shutterstock.com.

LIBRARY OF CONGRESS CATALOGING-IN-PUBLICATION DATA

Autism / Lauri S. Scherer, book editor.
    pages cm. -- (Introducing issues with opposing viewpoints)
  Summary: "Introducing Issues with Opposing Viewpoints: Autism: Introducing Issues with Opposing Viewpoints is a series that examines current issues from different viewpoints, set up in a pro/con format"-- Provided by publisher.
  Includes bibliographical references and index.
  ISBN 978-0-7377-6920-3 (hardback)
  1. Autism in children--Juvenile literature. 2. Autistic children--Juvenile literature.
 I. Scherer, Lauri S., editor of compilation.
  RJ506.A9A8698 2014
  618.92'85882--dc23
                                        2013026138

Printed in the United States of America
1 2 3 4 5 6 7 18 17 16 15 14

Contents

Chapter 3: How Can Autism Be Reduced, Treated, or Cured?

Foreword

Indulging in a wide spectrum of ideas, beliefs, and perspectives is a critical cornerstone of democracy. After all, it is often debates over differences of opinion, such as whether to legalize abortion, how to treat prisoners, or when to enact the death penalty, that shape our society and drive it forward. Such diversity of thought is frequently regarded as the hallmark of a healthy and civilized culture. As the Reverend Clifford Schutjer of the First Congregational Church in Mansfield, Ohio, declared in a 2001 sermon, "Surrounding oneself with only like-minded people, restricting what we listen to or read only to what we find agreeable is irresponsible. Refusing to entertain doubts once we make up our minds is a subtle but deadly form of arrogance." With this advice in mind, Introducing Issues with Opposing Viewpoints books aim to open readers' minds to the critically divergent views that comprise our world's most important debates.

Introducing Issues with Opposing Viewpoints simplifies for students the enormous and often overwhelming mass of material now available via print and electronic media. Collected in every volume is an array of opinions that captures the essence of a particular controversy or topic. Introducing Issues with Opposing Viewpoints books embody the spirit of nineteenth-century journalist Charles A. Dana's axiom: "Fight for your opinions, but do not believe that they contain the whole truth, or the only truth." Absorbing such contrasting opinions teaches students to analyze the strength of an argument and compare it to its opposition. From this process readers can inform and strengthen their own opinions, or be exposed to new information that will change their minds. Introducing Issues with Opposing Viewpoints is a mosaic of different voices. The authors are statesmen, pundits, academics, journalists, corporations, and ordinary people who have felt compelled to share their experiences and ideas in a public forum. Their words have been collected from newspapers, journals, books, speeches, interviews, and the Internet, the fastest growing body of opinionated material in the world.

Introducing Issues with Opposing Viewpoints shares many of the well-known features of its critically acclaimed parent series, Opposing Viewpoints. The articles are presented in a pro/con format, allowing readers to absorb divergent perspectives side by side. Active reading questions preface each viewpoint, requiring the student to approach the material thoughtfully and carefully. Useful charts, graphs, and cartoons supplement each article. A thorough introduction provides readers with crucial background on an issue. An annotated bibliography points the reader toward articles, books, and websites that contain additional information on the topic. An appendix of organizations to contact contains a wide variety of charities, nonprofit organizations, political groups, and private enterprises that each hold a position on the issue at hand. Finally, a comprehensive index allows readers to locate content quickly and efficiently.

Introducing Issues with Opposing Viewpoints is also significantly different from Opposing Viewpoints. As the series title implies, its presentation will help introduce students to the concept of opposing viewpoints and learn to use this material to aid in critical writing and debate. The series' four-color, accessible format makes the books attractive and inviting to readers of all levels. In addition, each viewpoint has been carefully edited to maximize a reader's understanding of the content. Short but thorough viewpoints capture the essence of an argument. A substantial, thought-provoking essay question placed at the end of each viewpoint asks the student to further investigate the issues raised in the viewpoint, compare and contrast two authors' arguments, or consider how one might go about forming an opinion on the topic at hand. Each viewpoint contains sidebars that include at-a-glance information and handy statistics. A Facts About section located in the back of the book further supplies students with relevant facts and figures.

Following in the tradition of the Opposing Viewpoints series, Greenhaven Press continues to provide readers with invaluable exposure to the controversial issues that shape our world. As John Stuart Mill once wrote: "The only way in which a human being can make some approach to knowing the whole of a subject is by hearing what can be said about it by persons of every variety of opinion and studying all modes in which it can be looked at by every character of mind. No wise man ever acquired his wisdom in any mode but this." It is to this principle that Introducing Issues with Opposing Viewpoints books are dedicated.

Introduction

Autism, a neurological disorder that affects the way children develop, socialize, and communicate, is often viewed as the pediatric crisis of the twenty-first century. According to the organization Autism Speaks, which takes its data from the Centers for Disease Control and Prevention, the autism rate has jumped more than 600 percent over several decades. In 2012, 1 in 88 children were diagnosed with autism. Some believe that, compared with the rate in 1975 (when 1 in 5,000 children received such a diagnosis), 1985 (when 1 in 2,500 did), 1995 (when 1 in 500 did), 2001 (when 1 in 250 did), 2007 (when 1 in 150 did), and 2010 (when 1 in 110 did), this rate indicates that autism is an epidemic that claims thousands more children with every passing year. Others believe the rising rates are due not to actual increased incidence of the disorder, but to mass overdiagnosis and confusion over what really constitutes autism. The only thing more controversial than autism's causes and its true rate of affliction is the effectiveness of methods used to treat it.

In searching for answers, wild theories have been proposed for how to treat autism or alleviate its symptoms. One theory that gained ground in 2012 was that injecting people with worms could alleviate autism symptoms. This was first publicized by Stewart Johnson, a father who was desperate to cure his son Lawrence's worsening autism. After reading about a potential link between autism and immune system deficiencies, Johnson had the idea to inject his son, under scientific supervision, with eggs from a parasitic worm known as *Trichuris suis*. This is a type of whipworm that is dangerous to pigs but not humans. There is some evidence that exposure to such parasites can have a positive effect on the immune system and reduce inflammation in the body, both of which are suggested, though unproven, causes of autism. After several injections, Johnson noticed a decrease in his son's autistic symptoms, particularly his repetitive behaviors, inflexibility, and irritability.

In 2013 scientists at New York's Albert Einstein College of Medicine and the biotech company Coronado Biosciences were further investigating this treatment by undertaking the first clinical trials to evaluate the effect of whipworm therapy on autistic individuals. Eric Hollander, the trial's head scientist, found many reasons to be optimistic. "The TSO

[*Trichuris suis* ova] is a naturally-occurring drug delivering device that can dampen the inflammatory response and decrease pro-inflammatory cytokines, which is something that keeps the inflammatory process going," he explains. "That's associated with certain symptoms we see in the autism disorder."[1] Others, however, view whipworm therapy as a desperate and even dangerous undertaking. "No data exist to support using them [parasitic worms] to treat or prevent autism," warns scientist and autism expert Emily Willingham, who points out that parasites typically cause more health problems than they solve. "Lest we handle this too lightly, I'll add that infections with parasitic worms afflict an estimated 740 million people and can cause anemia and malnutrition. Having a bunch of worms growing in your intestines generally isn't preferable to not having them there."[2] Whether whipworm therapy is a valid autism treatment remains to be seen.

Another outlandish autism treatment is chelation therapy, in which individuals undergo a procedure to have high levels of heavy metals removed from their body. Steeped in the theory that autism is caused by exposure to environmental metals such as mercury from vaccines or lead from tainted water, chelation therapy works by injecting or exposing a person to drugs that attach to lead, mercury, arsenic, and other metals and eliminate them from the body. Although chelation therapy has been endorsed by autism advocacy organizations like Jenny McCarthy's Generation Rescue and others who believe autism is caused by the metallic preservatives in vaccines, chelation therapy has been criticized as ineffective and even lethal. Side effects of chelation therapy can include vomiting, hypertension, abnormal heart rhythms, and dangerously low calcium levels, which can result in heart attack. In fact, this is what killed a five-year-old autistic boy in 2005, who suffered a fatal heart attack after several chelation treatments. Because of the serious risks and lack of scientific evidence on both chelation therapy and autism's link to vaccines, most experts do not advise chelation therapy, yet it is still attempted by parents who are frantic to cure their child's autism. "Parents of children with autism are desperate," says Howard Carpenter, the executive director of the Advisory Board on Autism and Related Disorders. "Some are willing to try anything."[3]

While chelation, worm, and other experimental therapies are unproven and controversial, more success has been had with applied behavioral analysis (ABA), perhaps the most widely recommended autism therapy available today. This is a kind of behavioral therapy that uses techniques to increase positive, wanted behaviors and reduce negative ones that interfere with learning and functioning. ABA therapists use specific and personalized tactics to break down skills into more manageable, learnable steps (which autistic children struggle with); give children multiple opportunities to learn the skill; reward them with positive attention; teach them skills to use in their real-world environments; and overcome other learning and communicative challenges posed by their autism. The American Academy of Pediatrics, the US surgeon general, and other credible parties have enthusiastically endorsed ABA therapy as a safe and effective autism treatment, and its success has been verified by numerous studies that show ABA techniques improve communication, social, play, self-care, school, and employment skills. The main downside of ABA therapy is that it is intensive and expensive: Some programs recommend between twenty-five and forty hours per week of therapy for several years, and it is not always covered by insurance programs.

How to treat autism, and whether it should be treated at all, is but one topic covered in *Introducing Issues with Opposing Viewpoints: Autism*. Readers will also consider what causes autism, whether there is an autism epidemic, how autism should be clinically defined, and how the government, society, and families should handle the prevalence of autism in contemporary society. Pro/con article pairs expose readers to the basic debates surrounding autism and encourage them to develop their own opinions on the topic.

Notes

1. Quoted in Jessica Ryen Doyle, "Study Looks at Worm Therapy to Treat Autism," Fox News, January 22, 2013. www.foxnews .com/health/2013/01/21/study-looks-at-worm-therapy-to-treat -autism/#ixzz201WkyZsa.
2. Emily Willingham, "Autism, Immunity, Inflammation, and the *New York Times*," *Emily Willingham* (blog), August 27, 2012. www.emilywillinghamphd.com/2012/08/autism-immunity -inflammation-and-new.html.
3. Quoted in Karen Kane and Virginia Linn, "Boy Dies During Autism Treatment," *Pittsburgh (PA) Post-Gazette,* August 25, 2005. www.post-gazette.com/stories/local/uncategorized/boy-dies -during-autism-treatment-597180.

Chapter 1

What Causes Autism?

Statistics reveal that women who experience severe inflammation while pregnant—either from infections or autoimmune disorders— are more likely to give birth to an autistic child.

Immune System Deficiencies May Cause Autism

"Several studies have linked immune system abnormalities to autism."

Paula Goines, Paul Ashwood, and Judy Van de Water

The authors are affiliated with the University of California at Davis (UC–Davis). Paula Goines is a graduate of UC–Davis and is a doctoral student in the immunology graduate group. Paul Ashwood is an assistant professor in the department of medical microbiology and immunology. Judy Van de Water is an associate professor in the department of internal medicine. In the following viewpoint the authors point to studies that show abnormally increased or decreased levels of various immune response cytokine proteins in autistic patients. Such abnormalities could affect neural development. However, it is not known whether such abnormalities are the cause or result of autism.

Paula Goines, Paul Ashwood, and Judy Van de Water, "Autism Spectrum Disorders and the Immune System," Autism Society of America, 2006. Reproduced with permission.

The exact cause of autism spectrum disorders (ASD) is not well understood. ASD is likely to involve a combination of genetic, immunological and environmental factors, and may encompass several diseases with distinct origins. Currently there are no biological markers for ASD, and diagnosis is based solely on behavioral criteria.

A recent, dramatic rise in the incidence of ASD has sparked an intense effort toward a greater understanding of the disease. Several studies have linked immune system abnormalities to autism. Aberrant immune activity during critical periods in development potentially could enhance neurological disorders. The following is a brief summary of the current research correlating ASD and immune dysfunction.

Cytokines

Cytokines are proteins made by immune cells that regulate the nature, intensity and length of an immune response. Additionally, cytokines are important in the development and health of the central nervous system (CNS). Thus, abnormal cytokine production during critical windows of brain development could have long-term effects on the health of the nervous system.

Increased levels of proinflammatory cytokines such as TNF-alpha, and decreased levels of anti-inflammatory cytokines such as IL-10 have been observed in children with ASD. Imbalanced levels of these cytokines can augment inflammation and cause excess damage to tissues.

Cytokines secreted by T cells can be categorized into two major subsets termed TH1 (associated with a cell response and inflammation) and TH2 (associated with allergies and asthma). One study found elevated proportions of TH2-producing lymphocytes in subjects with ASD when compared with controls.

However, another study demonstrated a TH1-skewed cytokine profile. A third study found increased levels of both TH1 and TH2 cytokines without a compensatory increase of the regulatory cytokine IL-10 in a small group of ASD children. These contrasting findings may

The prevalence of inflammatory diseases in general has increased significantly in the past sixty years. As a group, they include asthma, now estimated to affect one in ten children—at least double the prevalence in 1980—and autoimmune disorders, which afflict one in twenty.

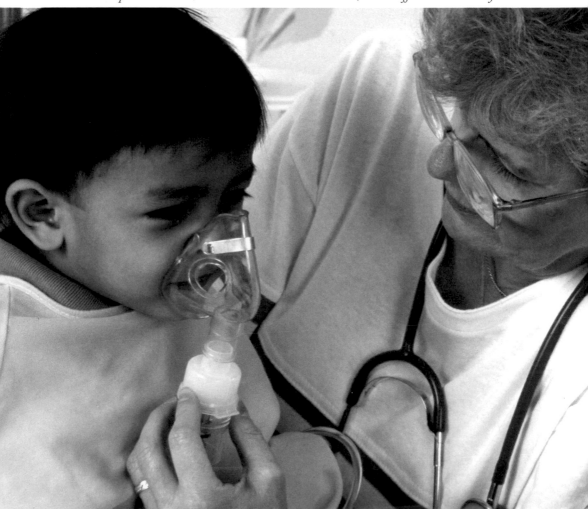

represent different categories of ASD, a theory that may be explored by taking behavioral characteristics into account.

The CNS contains different cell types that have a role both in brain function and the CNS immune response. A study in 2005 of brains from people with ASD showed inflammation characterized by activation of these specialized brain cells. Additionally, altered cytokine patterns were observed in the brains and cerebrospinal fluid of subjects with autism compared to controls. Abnormal immune responses in these brain cells in people with ASD may influence neural function and development, and could indicate an attempt by the activated cells to repair CNS damage.

Autoimmunity

Autoimmunity is a condition where a person's immune system is unable to differentiate "self" from "nonself" components. In such cases, the immune system develops "self reactive" antibodies and/or cells that lead an attack against the body's own tissues as if they were foreign invaders. Autoimmunity is well defined in diseases such as rheumatoid arthritis and systemic lupus. However, autoimmune reactions to brain tissues also may be involved in a subset of autism cases. The presence of antibodies to brain tissues is abnormal and can be detrimental to CNS development and function.

> ## FAST FACT
>
> Vijendra K. Singh, a neuroimmunology professor at Utah State University, maintains that up to 80 percent of autism cases are caused by abnormal immune system reactions.

Several studies have demonstrated the presence of autoantibodies specific to various CNS tissues in subjects with autism and animal models, including myelin basic protein, neuronal and glial filament proteins, and several other unidentified brain antigens. These studies show that autoimmune activity can be associated with autism in some (but not all) cases. It is difficult to determine whether these autoantibodies contribute to the development of the disorder or if they are a consequence of the disease.

Americans Are Very Concerned About Autism

A poll by the National Alliance on Autism Research shows sizable numbers of Americans are concerned about autism and the effect it might have on their families, even though there is considerable debate about what causes it.

71%
say they are concerned about autism.

87%
say autism is a very serious problem.

19%
have been concerned at some point that their child or a relative's child has autism.

27%
of parents worry their child or grandchild might develop autism.

Taken from: National Alliance for Autism Research.

Gastrointestinal Immunity

Gastrointestinal (GI) symptoms, including abdominal pain, bloating, diarrhea and constipation have been reported in a subset of subjects with ASD. Those with GI symptoms have been found to have inflammatory cytokine profiles in mucosal immune cells and peripheral blood compared to controls. The exact relationship between GI symptoms and ASD is unclear. The GI tract is the site of extensive and specific immune activity, and it has been proposed that immune-mediated GI pathology may lead to systemic immune activation and inflammation in the brain. However, there is yet to be concrete data to support this claim.

Conclusion

There appears to be a strong correlation between immune dysfunction and autism, though the extent to which aberrant immune activity is involved in the pathogenesis of autism is unknown. ASD must be recognized as a spectrum of diseases, each of which may have a distinct cause and disease process. Future research should focus on finding biological markers for ASD and its variations. This breakthrough would open the door for early testing and intervention during the first few years of life, a time that is critical for brain and neural development.

EVALUATING THE AUTHOR'S ARGUMENTS:

The authors, Paula Goines, Paul Ashwood, and Judy Van de Water, point to studies that show abnormal levels of immune response proteins called cytokines in patients with autism. Do you think it is more likely that these abnormal levels are a cause or a result of autism? Why?

"Correlations have been found between autism and a dizzying number of variables. . . . It's easy to cherry pick the observations that support the inflammation hypothesis of autism and ignore the others."

Is Autism a Prenatal Parasite-Deficiency Syndrome?

Lindsay Beyerstein

Autism is not likely caused by immune system deficiencies, argues Lindsay Beyerstein in the following viewpoint. She considers arguments made by Moises Velasquez-Manoff who contends that a lack of exposure to parasites increases inflammation and the prevalence of autoimmune disorders, which in turn causes autism. But Beyerstein argues that many of Velasquez-Manoff's observations are not universally true. For example, Velasquez-Manoff says people in developing nations have lower rates of both inflammatory disease and autism; but Beyerstein says high rates of both infection and autoimmune inflammatory disease (such as asthma) exist in developing countries. Furthermore, she says, low rates of autism in such places could be explained by a lack of diagnosis, not necessarily a lack of presence of the condition. Beyerstein agrees that there is something to the idea that an overly "clean" society devoid of parasites could contribute to increased inflammation and autoimmune disease, but she says there is not nearly enough evidence to link this idea to autism. Beyerstein analyzes news, media, culture, and politics for *Duly Noted*, a blog published by *In These Times*.

AS YOU READ, CONSIDER THE FOLLOWING QUESTIONS:
1. What does the author note about children in South America? What bearing does it have on her argument?
2. Why might children be less likely to be diagnosed with autism in developing countries, according to Beyerstein?
3. What, says Beyerstein, is an ongoing challenge for the immune system?

I f you're the sort of parent who throws "chickenpox parties," please stop reading now. I don't want you to get the idea that your daughter needs a good, old fashioned case of hookworm to ward off autism in her future offspring. The War on Women is fierce enough without people thinking that today's uppity broads don't have enough parasites to bear strapping young.

That said, Moises Velasquez-Manoff has a provocative op/ed in the *New York Times* about a possible link between decreased rates of parasitic infections and increased rates of inflammatory diseases like arthritis, allergies, and possibly even autism. The piece has been hovering near the top of the site's "most read" list for days.

Biologist and science writer Emily Willingham offers a much-needed skeptical corrective to Velasquez-Manoff's argument. She notes that Velasquez-Manoff seems way more confident about what causes autism than the world's autism experts. Correlations have been found between autism and a dizzying number of variables, ranging from paternal age to environmental pollution to allergies and asthma during pregnancy. It's easy to cherry pick the observations that support the inflammation hypothesis of autism and ignore the others.

Velasquez-Manoff argues that prenatal inflammation causes up to a third of all cases of autism and that much of this inflammation is caused by a dearth of parasites in the mother.

This idea is based on the off-hand observation that countries with high rates of parasitic infection seem to have lower rates of asthma, allergies, inflammatory bowel syndrome, and other chronic infammatory illnesses that plague many people in the industrialized West, not to mention lower rates of autism. Willingham questions the premise that people in developing countries are less prone to inflammatory diseases or autism. She notes that children in South America have both high rates of parasitic infection and high rates of athsma. Autism in developing countries may be more common than it appears because children are less likely to be diagnosed; either because they have less access to health care or because other cultures categorize their atypical behaviors differently than American parents and doctors do.

Parasites are hardly the only difference between impoverished people in the Global South and well-off folks in the Global North, and correlation should never be casually equated with causation.

However, the evolutionary biology of host-parasite interactions suggests there may be something to the idea that abolishing parasites set the stage for inflammatory diseases. Autism is a long shot because it's not clear that inflammation causes autism. But there are many clear-cut inflammatory/ autoimmune diseases that might be more plausibly explained by the so-called Hygiene Hypothesis.

Inflammation defends the body against infection and trauma, but it can also injure healthy tissue. Keeping up a vigorous defense while minimizing friendly fire casualties is a perennial challenge for the immune system.

Some parasites have evolved to suppress the inflammatory response of their host. This makes sense, because inflammation is one way

> **FAST FACT**
>
> A 2010 study published in the *Journal of Autism and Developmental Disorders* found that just 1.5 percent of all children with autism spectrum disorder had mothers who came down with infections during pregnancy. Although researchers did conclude that infection during the first trimester significantly increased the risk of a child developing autism, 98.5 percent of all cases were considered to be unrelated to prenatal maternal infection.

the body fights off parasites. Parasites that can dampen down host defenses are more likely to stay put and produce baby parasites.

By the same token, hosts that can muster a vigorous immune response and at least keep the infestation down to manageable level are more likely to produce baby hosts. If the human immune system is designed for constant low-level warfare against parasites that dampen the immune system, what happens when improved sanitation trounces the parasites once and for all? Could the historically novel absence of immune-dampening parasites leave our tissues vulnerable to the full power of our own immune systems?

Humans and their intestinal worms came up together. The evolutionary history of one species is inscribed on the other. What looked like an abusive relationship may turn out to have been codependency. Researchers are hard at work probing the relationship between intestinal worms, or lack thereof, and inflammatory bowel disease.

In the industrial era, entire societies have become virtually parasite-free, but only a fraction of the population succumbs to auto-immune disease, so there must be other factors at play. Willingham presents genetic and environmental factors as possible alternative explanations for putative increase in certain ailments, but we can also see the Hygiene Hypothesis as potentially complimentary.

It's too bad that Velasquez-Manoff overstates the case for autism because it detracts from a fascinating, though unproven, hypothesis about the origins of chronic inflammatory diseases.

EVALUATING THE AUTHOR'S ARGUMENTS:

To make her argument, Lindsay Beyerstein alludes to the "hygiene hypothesis" but does not fully detail what that is. Using the other viewpoints in this book or the resources in your school or public library, research the hygiene hypothesis and write one to two paragraphs detailing both what it is and what connection it has, if any, to autism.

Vaccines Might Cause Autism

Kent Heckenlively

"The idea of an underlying retrovirus was the first time it made sense as to how a vaccination might cause autism."

Kent Heckenlively is a contributing editor to *Age of Autism*, a daily newspaper on the Internet. In the following viewpoint the author suggests that vaccination of a person infected with a retrovirus might cause autism. Stimulation of the immune system of a person infected with a retrovirus, as with a vaccine, can cause the retrovirus to replicate out of control. The immune system is already compromised by the retrovirus, and the stimulation places greater demand on that system. Heavy metals, such as mercury, used in vaccines could exacerbate this response.

AS YOU READ, CONSIDER THE FOLLOWING QUESTIONS:

1. As reported by the author, how is HIV accelerated by vaccinations?
2. According to the author, what was a likely cause of neurosyphilis?
3. As stated in the article, autism shares many common clinical features with what other conditions?

When my daughter's test results showed she was positive for the XMRV (xenotropic murine leukemia virus related virus) retrovirus my next step was to find a doctor who could tell me how to treat it. Since the only other two human retroviruses currently identified are HTLV [human T-cell lymphotropic virus], found mostly in Asian countries and responsible for causing T-cell leukemia, and HIV, which causes AIDS, I figured I had to find an AIDS doctor.

I called the University of California, San Francisco [UCSF] Pediatric AIDS unit and talked to their media representative. I figured in our first conversation I'd avoid flying my freak flag and simply tell him my daughter had been diagnosed with this newly identified retrovirus and that she had autism and seizures and I was concerned that the retrovirus might be at least partially responsible for her problems.

"Well, that explains why a vaccination might cause autism," he said, barely missing a breath. He went on to tell me this question was something he often discussed with his friends. The idea of an underlying retrovirus was the first time it made sense as to how a vaccination might cause autism.

He explained that if XMRV was similar to HIV then it probably hid out in the cells of the immune system and any stimulation of the immune system was likely to cause XMRV to replicate out of control. (This had previously been discussed by some of the researchers working on XMRV, but I was still surprised to hear the media representative go right to that point.) Apparently it is common knowledge among retrovirologists that immunizations can stimulate a retrovirus. Even the most pro-vaccine physician will admit that vaccinations work by stimulating the immune system.

The media representative was very kind and said he'd try to find a doctor to talk to me. Predictably, none of them wanted to talk to me, and I can't say I'm unsatisfied with that result. The currently existing HIV medications don't hold much appeal to me as I worry about some of their side-effects, particularly on the mitochondria.

I've avoided writing this story for the better part of the year since I couldn't find any confirmation of what the media representative had told me. And it was a BIG thing to say without confirmation.

I was reading a chronic fatigue/ME [myalgic encephalomyelitis] forum the other day and came across my long-sought confirmation. It's actually on the University of California, San Francisco website for HIV and you can read it HERE [URL not shown].

The article is entitled "Immunizations and HIV" and it had some interesting observations. In the section on the "Effect of Vaccines on HIV Disease Progression" was the following paragraph.

"Activation of the cellular immune system is important in the pathogenesis of HIV disease, and that fact has given rise to concerns that activation of the immune system through vaccinations might accelerate the progression of HIV disease. Activation of CD4 lymphocytes, which takes place when these cells respond to an antigenic stimulus, makes those cells more susceptible to HIV infection. Activated CD4 cells, once they become infected, support replication of HIV. Resting CD4 cells, although less susceptible, also are vulnerable to HIV infection. Replication of HIV in these cells is restricted, however, until immunologic activation occurs, at which time active HIV replication is initiated. These observations suggest that activation of the immune system through vaccinations could accelerate the progression of HIV disease through enhanced HIV replication."

Translation for the average person—HIV really kicks into high gear when the immune system is stimulated. And what are we doing with our current vaccination schedule except stimulating the immune system, even on the first day of life with the hepatitis B shot? And when you add to this equation the findings that about 3–7% of the healthy population carries this retrovirus the size of this potential problem becomes much more clear.

I can't think of a better example of how vaccines, their heavy metals (because of the havoc they play with the immune system's ability to deal with pathogens) and particularly mercury, might exacerbate a previously existing pathogen, and make the course of a disease much worse, than the section which opens up *The Age of Autism* by Dan Olmsted and Mark Blaxill. They begin by discussing syphilis, which is caused by a bacterium of the *Treponema pallidium* species of the spirochete order. While the disease initially caused death in a few months to the Europeans who contracted it after it was apparently brought back from the New World, it then evolved into a less pathogenic, but more chronic disease.

A cruelly-debilitating condition which became known as "neuro-syphilis" or "general paralysis of the insane" started to be reported in the early 1800s. The authors indeed refer to it as akin to "AIDS before retroviral therapy." Mercury had long been known to treat skin disorders, and since one of the maladies of syphilis were terrible lesions, doctors in Europe began treating syphilis with mercury. Olmsted and Blaxill link the rise of neuro-syphilis to this use of mercury, also pointing out the near absence of the condition in communities which did not use mercurial treatments.

The use of penicillin, starting in the late 1940s and early 1950s effectively short-circuited further inquiry into the question of what role mercury might have played in the development of neuro-syphilis. Penicillin went after the spirochette bacterium, and that was all anybody seemed to care about.

I make this digression because I don't want it to be misunderstood that since I'm talking about a retrovirus I think that some of the other vaccine components don't play a role. I do think they make the condition worse. Mercury, aluminum salts, and many other components have not been fully tested for safety, and as a parent, that is appalling to me. Much has been written on these subjects, though, and my intention in this article is to open up new areas of inquiry.

Further on in the UCSF informational article on immunizations and HIV is the following observation, "In general, it is prefeable to avoid live-virus vaccines if an alternative inactivated vaccine is avail-

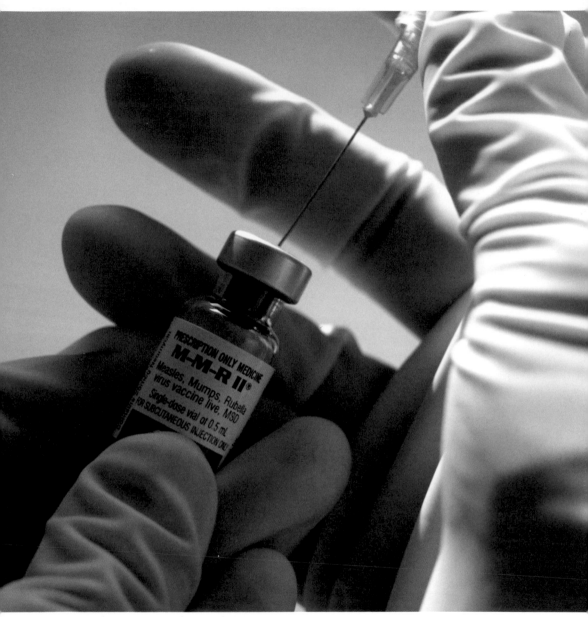

The author mentions that the MMR vaccine is a live-virus vaccine that could pose a risk to patients with compromised immune systems.

able. . . . There are several reports of severe illness or death involving HIV-infected individuals after live-virus vaccination."

In the discussion of the measles, mumps, and rubella shots the UCSF article makes the following statements, "Live vaccines are used for MMR [measles, mumps, and rubella] and thus may pose risks in

A 2011 poll found a slim majority of Americans believed there was no connection between vaccines and autism. Nearly half were either unsure or thought there was a connection.

Question:
"The theory that vaccines can cause autism is . . ."

Not True—52%*		Not Sure or True—48%		
Certainly Not True	Probably Not True	Not Sure	Probably True	Certainly True
20%	31%	30%	16%	2%

*Percentages do not add up due to rounding.

Taken from: Harris Interactive/HealthDay, January 20, 2011.

immunocompromised patients . . . As with other vaccines, serologic response may be poor in HIV infection, and children with severe HIV-related immunosuppression should be considered susceptible to measles even if they have received measles vaccine . . . There have been case reports of fatal pneumonitis after measles vaccination in severely immunocompromised adults, and response to vaccine appears to be poor."

Translation—Live virus vaccines such as MMR seem to cause trouble if you're already infected with a retrovirus. I've written previously that my daughter, my wife, and my mother-in-law have all tested positive for XMRV while I have tested negative. And if you do have a retrovirus, and get a vaccination, and don't have any problems, you may still get illnesses like the measles because your immune system isn't responding properly. Could this be behind some of the increase in measles infections, even among those children who have been vaccinated?

I've written before that XMRV may be linked to autism as it has been shown to integrate preferentially at the start site of genes and in

CpG islands [genomic regions that contain a high frequency of CpG, phosphodiester bonds between the cytosine and the guanine]. This could explain a number of the methylation pattern changes seen in autism. Retroviruses can also affect mitochondrial function through the production of reactive oxygen and nitrogen species. Autism shares many common clinical features with other conditions, such as chronic fatigue syndrome/ME, including immune disregulation, increased expression of pro-inflammatory cytokines and chemokines, and chronic active microbial infections.

I've also written before how in a small study 14 out of 17 (82%) of children with autism were found to test positive for the XMRV retrovirus. A poster presentation of this research was made approximately a year ago at the 1st International Workshop on XMRV held at the National Institutes of Health in Bethesda, Maryland on September 7 and 8, 2010.

The issue of XMRV raises many questions, not the least of which is how to treat it. If HIV is any guide to treatment, then it seems any attempt to increase the function of the immune system may result in further viral replication. It seems to me the virus itself would first need to be attacked, although I can't see anything on the market at the current time that is both effective, and relatively safe.

It does have the potential to answer some of our most vexing questions, though. Namely, what about those children who acquired autism, but were only partially or never vaccinated. Could that also explain why those cases tend to be relatively mild? The mercury and other heavy metals in the vaccine may not have had the chance to make the infection worse.

Many questions remain about XMRV, but they are important questions for our country, and should be the subject of serious research. We need virologists and retrovirologists in the medical community to use their knowledge and moral courage to help us put together the pieces of this puzzle. If we work together I believe the answers to our questions may be closer than we realize.

For further information on how a vaccination could activate a retrovirus you might want to consult these articles which were kindly provided to me by a member of the chronic fatigue syndrome/ME community.

- T cell activation and human immunodeficiency virus replication after influenza immunization of infected children—Ramilo et al The Pediatric infectious disease journal 1996, vol. 15, no3, pp. 197-203 (25 ref.) Clin Biochem
- Activation of virus replication after vaccination of HIV-1-infected individuals—Staprans SI et al J Exp Med. 1995 Dec 1;182(6):1727-37.
- Transient increases in numbers of infectious cells in an HIV-infected chimpanzee following immune stimulation—Fultz PN et al AIDS Res Hum Retroviruses. 1992 Feb;8(2):313-7.
- Human immunodeficiency virus-type 1 replication can be increased in peripheral blood of seropositive patients after influenza vaccination. O'Brien WA et al Blood. 1995 Aug 1;86(3):1082-9.
- Measles/MMR vaccine for infants born to HIV-positive mothers [Intervention Protocol], B Unnikrishnan et al, The Cochrane Library 2009, Issue 1
- Effect of immunization with a common recall antigen on viral expression in patients infected with human immunodeficiency virus type 1—Stanley SK et al N Engl J Med. 1996 May 9;334(19):1222-30.
- The efficiency of acute infection of CD4+ T cells is markedly enhanced in the setting of antigen-specific immune activation—Weissman D et al J Exp Med. 1996 Feb 1;183(2):687-92.
- Antigenic stimulation by BCG vaccine as an in vivo driving force for SIV replication and dissemination—Cheynier Really et al. Nat Med. 1998 Apr;4(4):421-7.
- Activation by malaria antigens renders mononuclear cells susceptible to HIV infection and re-activates replication of endogenous HIV in cells from HIV-infected adults—Froebel K et al Parasite Immunol. 2004 May;26(5):213-7.

EVALUATING THE AUTHOR'S ARGUMENTS:

The author, Kent Heckenlively, connects issues related to HIV and vaccination to autism and the XMRV retrovirus. What parts of his argument do you find the most convincing? The least convincing? Why?

Vaccines Not Associated with Risk of Autism

Centers for Disease Control and Prevention

"A new study . . . adds to the conclusion . . . by the Institute of Medicine (IOM) that there is not a causal relationship between certain vaccine types and autism."

Centers for Disease Control and Prevention (CDC) is the health protection agency of the US government. In the following viewpoint the author reports on a new study that found the number of antigens received from vaccines to cause the immune system to fight disease was the same in both autistic and non-autistic children.

AS YOU READ, CONSIDER THE FOLLOWING QUESTIONS:

1. As reported by the author, the study reviewed data from how many children with autism and how many children without autism?
2. According to the author, what is ASD with regression?
3. According to the article, how many vaccine antigens were given by two years of age in the 1990s? In 2013?

Centers for Disease Control and Prevention, "Vaccines Not Associated with Risk of Autism," www.cdc.gov /vaccinesafety/Concerns/Autism/antigens.html.

A new study evaluating parents' concerns of "too many vaccines too soon" and autism has been published online in the *Journal of Pediatrics*, March 29, 2013. It adds to the conclusion of a 2004 comprehensive review by the Institute of Medicine (IOM) that there is not a causal relationship between certain vaccine types and autism. The results provide relevant data for the current childhood immunization schedule.

The study looked at the amount of antigens from vaccines received on one day of vaccination and the amount of antigens from vaccines received in total during the first two years of life and found no connection to the development of autism spectrum disorder (ASD) in children. Antigens are substances in vaccines that cause the body's immune system to produce antibodies to fight disease.

Researchers collected data from 3 managed care organizations in a group of 256 children with ASD compared with 752 children without ASD.

The study's main findings report:

- The total amount of antigens from vaccines received was the same between children with ASD and those that did not have ASD.
- Children with ASD with regression (the loss of developmental skills during the second year of life) did not receive an increased number of vaccine antigens when compared to children without ASD with regression.
- The number of vaccine antigens has decreased in recent years. Although the routine childhood vaccine immunization schedule in 2013 contains more vaccines than the schedule in the late 1990s, the maximum number of vaccine antigens that a child would be exposed to by 2 years of age in 2013 is 315, compared with several thousand in the late 1990s. This is due to changes

in the vaccines. For example, the older whole cell pertussis vaccine causes the body to produce about 3,000 different antibodies, whereas the newer acellular pertussis vaccines cause the production of 6 or fewer different antibodies.

An infant's immune system is capable of responding to a large amount of immunologic stimuli and, from time of birth, infants are exposed to hundreds of viruses and countless antigens that are not associated with vaccination. This study demonstrates that autism spectrum disorder is not associated with immunological stimulation from vaccines during the first 2 years of life.

The author contends that numerous international studies have repeatedly disproven any link between autism and vaccinations.

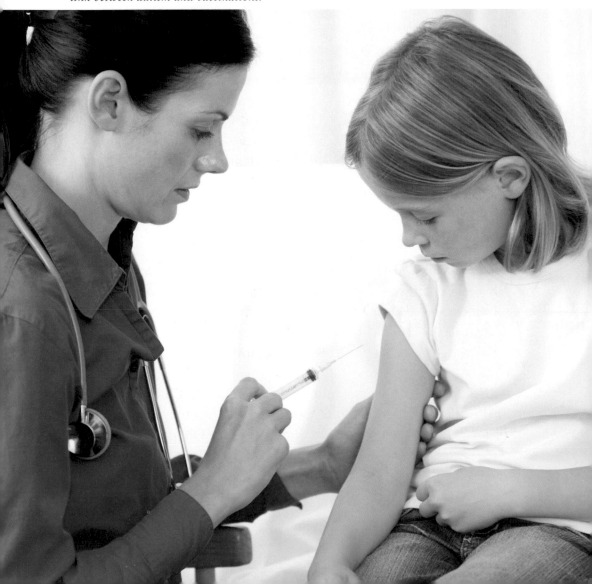

Parents should expect the vaccines their children receive are safe and effective. CDC [Centers for Disease Control and Prevention], along with other federal agencies, is committed to assuring the safety of vaccines through rigorous pre-licensure trials and post-licensure monitoring.

EVALUATING THE AUTHOR'S ARGUMENTS:

The author, Centers for Disease Control and Prevention, supports the conclusion that vaccines do not cause autism, based on the study that found that the number of antigens received was the same for both those with and without ASD. How do you think the author of the previous viewpoint, Kent Heckenlively, would respond to this argument?

Autism Risk Rises with Father's Age

Gautam Naik

"'It's very likely that the rise in the mean age of fathers has made some contribution to the apparent epidemic of autism in our society.'"

In the following viewpoint Gautam Naik reports on evidence that autism is caused in part by a father's age at the time of his child's conception. He explains that unlike eggs, which exist inside a woman even before her birth, sperm is constantly regenerated by the male body. Undergoing numerous cell divisions throughout a man's reproductive life makes sperm prone to error and genetic mutation, especially as a man ages. Naik reports that the sperm of older men can contain more than twice the number of genetic errors as their younger counterparts, which likely explains why the offspring of older men are more likely to suffer from autism and other neurological conditions. He concludes the increase in autism rates could be explained by the increasing numbers of men who become fathers at older ages. Naik is a reporter for the *Wall Street Journal*, where this article was originally published in August 2012.

*S*tudy finds older dads are more likely to pass on harmful genetic mutations.

Older fathers pass on more new genetic mutations to their children than younger fathers, increasing their children's risk of autism, schizophrenia and other diseases, new research published Wednesday shows.

While advanced maternal age is a major cause behind rare chromosomal problems such as Down syndrome in babies, the latest findings add to growing evidence suggesting that at conception it is the father's age—rather than the mother's—that is the main factor behind the passing of new hereditary mutations to children.

> **FAST FACT**
>
> Swedish researchers have concluded that a father's risk of having a child with autism begins to rise when he is thirty years old and that men over fifty-five are four times more likely than those under thirty to father an autistic child.

The research was based on a genetic analysis of 78 Icelandic families with offspring who had a diagnosis of autism or schizophrenia. The data was published Wednesday in the journal *Nature*.

"It's very likely that the rise in the mean age of fathers has made some contribution to the apparent epidemic of autism in our society," said Kari Stefansson, chief executive officer of deCODE Genetics in Iceland and lead author of the study.

Studies of people in Iceland and elsewhere have indicated the risk of both autism and schizophrenia increase significantly with the father's age at conception. The average age of new Icelandic fathers is 33 and on the rise—as is the case in many Western countries.

The latest paper focuses on spontaneous changes in genetic coding known as de novo—or new—mutations.

These errors aren't inherited from the parental lineage. Instead, these mistakes occur only in eggs or sperm cells, or just after fertilization. In such cases, children will carry a genetic mutation in every cell without there being any family history of that particular alteration.

Sperm pick up more of these genetic spelling errors because, unlike eggs, they are constantly produced and go through many more cell divisions. Sperm from older men carry more errors.

Most of these mutations likely have little health impact; only a few are harmful and contribute to diseases.

Occasionally, a de novo mutation can be beneficial. Such alterations—which generate the diversity on which selection can act—are the essence of human evolution.

"The old father is dangerous to his children but can be beneficial to the future of the species," said Dr. Stefansson of DeCode, a biotechnology firm and major funder of the study.

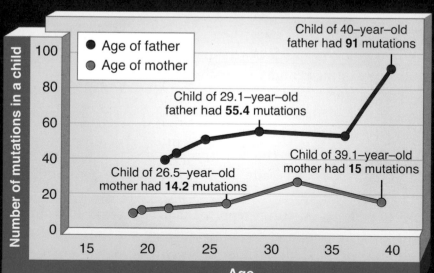

A Biological Clock for Men?

New research shows that children of older fathers have more new genetic mutations than do children of older mothers.

● Age of father
● Age of mother

Child of 40–year–old father had **91** mutations

Child of 29.1–year–old father had **55.4** mutations

Child of 26.5–year–old mother had **14.2** mutations

Child of 39.1–year–old mother had **15** mutations

Number of mutations in a child

100
80
60
40
20
0

15   20   25   30   35   40

Age

Studies of people in Iceland and elsewhere have indicated that the risk to a newborn of developing both autism and schizophrenia increases significantly if the father is over fifty.

Previous studies that unearthed similar associations between late fatherhood and a rise in de novo mutations were based on an analysis of about 1% of the genome. The latest work confirms those findings and "extends them to the other 99% of the genome," said Stephan Sanders, a geneticist at Yale University, who wasn't involved in the *Nature* paper.

A deleterious de novo error can especially affect brain functioning in children. That may be because more genes are expressed in the brain than in any other organ.

Several years ago, scientists reported that a man over 40 is almost six times as likely as a man under 30 to father an autistic child. Research has also shown that kids of older fathers are at higher risk of schizophrenia, bipolarity and epilepsy. One 2009 study suggested a link between late fatherhood and weaker performance by children in intelligence tests.

The *Nature* paper showed that the father's age at the time a child is conceived accounts for the vast majority of new mutations found in the offspring.

It also found that while a 20-year-old dad passes on an average of 25 new genetic spelling errors to his child, a father twice his age transmits about 65. Thus, every additional year of paternal age results in an average of two extra mutations in offspring.

A mother, meanwhile, transmits a constant rate of about 14 de novo errors to a child, regardless of her age.

A comprehensive genetic analysis like this would have been difficult to do just a few years ago. However, because it is easier now to sequence the entire genomes of people, scientists can probe our genetic workings in great detail.

Dr. Stefansson's team sequenced the genomes of 78 Icelandic families—parents and offspring—or a total of 219 individuals. Of the children, 44 have autism spectrum disorder and 21 are schizophrenic. The team also sequenced the genomes of 1,859 other Icelanders for comparison purposes.

EVALUATING THE AUTHOR'S ARGUMENTS:

Because of the fact that women eventually stop menstruating, it has long been known they have a finite window to have children, especially healthy ones. But the research presented in this viewpoint suggests that men, too, might have limits on the years they are able to produce healthy children. In addition to the biological implications of this research, what political or social implications do you think it poses? In what way might the existence of a male "biological clock" change the way in which men date, marry, start families, or organize their careers? Consider these issues in two to three paragraphs on the subject.

Women's Changing Social Role Can Explain the Rise in Autism

Michael Hanlon

"When people with strongly 'systemising' personalities . . . marry each other and produce children, the effects of this kind of 'male brain' are genetically magnified, increasing the chances of producing an autistic child."

In the following viewpoint Michael Hanlon suggests that the changing social role of women has contributed to the rise in autism. He explains that over the past century, women have become more educated and employed as doctors, engineers, scientists, and computer experts. As a result, they increasingly marry men of the same professions, and thus the couple shares traits particular to these professions and personality types, such as obsessiveness, perfectionism, and social awkwardness. Hanlon says the children of such a couple will exhibit these traits to an extreme, which could account for their autism. Whereas in the past doctors might marry nurses or scientists might marry secretaries, Hanlon says such men increasingly want a partner who is their equal. The unintended consequence of their unions might be more children with genetic tendencies toward the kind of traits associated with autism. Hanlon is a science journalist and blogger for the *Daily Mail*, a British newspaper.

AS YOU READ, CONSIDER THE FOLLOWING QUESTIONS:
1. What does the phrase "extreme male brain" mean in the context of the viewpoint?
2. What has occurred in the Silicon Valley in California, and how does it factor into the author's argument?
3. Why, according to Hanlon, is it significant that pilots, who used to marry stewardesses, now marry other pilots?

The autism epidemic seen in most Western countries in the past 30 years is one of the great medical mysteries of our time. The cause cannot be some great genetic shift—there simply hasn't been enough time for this to have happened.

Our diets are not hugely different and there is nothing to suggest any other aspect of our lifestyles might be to blame.

One rather bizarre hypothesis, that certain combinations of vaccines given to toddlers might be to blame, has now been thoroughly discredited.

One 'explanation' is certainly over diagnosis; fifty years ago 'autism' was quite narrowly defined, a serious mental impairment which normally prevented sufferers taking a place in mainstream society.

Now children who are simply a bit obsessive or who show signs of social dysfunction are routinely labelled 'autistic spectrum' or 'Asperger's'.

But over diagnosis cannot explain all the rise—from one-in-2500 in the United States to around 1 per cent today (and similar rates in the UK).

Mating Trends Could Explain Autism Rise

For some years now Professor Simon Baron-Cohen (cousin of the comedian and actor Sacha), a psychologist at Cambridge University, has been developing his theory that something called 'assortative mating' may be at least partly to blame for the spectacular rise in autism diagnoses.

The theory states that when people with strongly 'systemising' personalities—the sort of people who become engineers, surgeons, computer experts and who shine in some aspects of business—marry each other and produce children, the effects of this kind of 'male brain' are genetically magnified, increasing the chances of producing an autistic child—a child with what Prof Baron-Cohen suspects is an 'extreme male brain'.

Strong 'systemisers' are often slightly obsessive, perfectionist and make great scientists and are often extremely talented at music. But they sometimes have difficulties socially interacting with other people— a combination of traits that can blend into the milder end of the autism spectrum.

When Systemisers Marry Systemisers

Cambridge University's Autism Research Centre is now asking members of the public who are graduates and parents to take part in a survey which will investigate any links between educational achievement, what kind of job they have and how their children develop.

Specifically, the new study will attempt to find out whether two 'strong systemisers' do indeed have a higher chance of producing autistic children.

Prof Baron-Cohen's theory is certainly plausible.

Some of the sharpest increases in autism diagnoses have been found in Silicon Valley, in California—home to perhaps the largest population of successful systemisers on Earth, the tens of thousands of technicians, engineers and programmers who work in the computer industry. Inevitably, many of these people marry each other (there are now plenty of women working in IT, not the case a generation ago) and this is good (although circumstantial) evidence of the systemising-autism link.

The Rise of Female Brainpower

But what about other places? Why the rise in autism just about everywhere? One answer could be the changing role of women in general seen in the last 100 years.

Until relatively recently in our history, being exceptionally bright was not much use to you if you were female. In Victorian Britain, for example, the opportunities for a woman to earn her living through brainpower alone were extremely limited.

According to the 1901 Census, there were fewer than a hundred registered female doctors in the whole of the United Kingdom.

Going to university was difficult and expensive—most did not even allow girls to study. There were certainly few opportunities for careers in engineering or the sciences.

You could become a teacher or a governess, or maybe, if you were exceptionally talented, earn your living writing or in the arts. Most of the professions were closed, as was the world of business.

Brainy women were not even seen as particularly desirable partners. Clever or rich men chose brides on the grounds of looks, 'breeding' or both.

Having an IQ in the 140s probably counted against you if anything. The traditional image of a 'dumb blonde' hanging off the arm of the successful politician or businessman was a horrible cliché but it had an element of truth.

And in any case, very clever women would have often been mad to get married.

Alpha Males Want Alpha Females

Until the 1880s British women who wed could not even own their own property.

If . . . she did have a job, many employers would automatically sack a girl the moment she turned up with an engagement ring. So many clever, 'systemising' women simply did not marry, or married late—and probably had fewer children when they did.

Now everything has changed. Not only have the legal and social barriers to women entering the workplace as equals been largely dismantled, we also have the phenomenon of the desirable 'alpha female'. Fifty years ago many men were scared of smart women. Now, increasingly, alpha males want someone their equal or even superior.

Fifty years ago, male airline pilots typically married stewardesses; now they marry other pilots. Doctors used to marry nurses; now they marry other doctors.

The wives of successful politicians are, increasingly, successful in their own right—and of course many successful politicians are women.

Prof Baron-Cohen points out that 'alpha females' are not necessarily strong systemisers.

Being a brilliant politician or writer may not require the sort of geeky 'male brain' that may lie behind the autism rise.

But the phenomenon of like-marrying-like may be having completely unexpected consequences that go far beyond mere equal opportunities for women.

It is a fascinating theory and we await the results of the new study with interest.

EVALUATING THE AUTHOR'S ARGUMENTS:

In this viewpoint Michael Hanlon reports on the theory of assortative mating, which argues that women's increase in status, education, and profession—coupled with men's increasing desire to have a partner who is their intellectual and professional equal—has contributed to the increase in autism. What is your opinion of this theory? Is it plausible? What kind of evidence supports it? If true, what social, economic, or political implications might it have?

Chapter 2

How Serious Is the Problem of Autism?

Whether autism has become epidemic is hotly debated.

There Is an Autism Epidemic

Denise D. Resnik

In the following viewpoint Denise D. Resnik argues there are so many cases of autism in the United States that it constitutes an epidemic. She says over the past twenty years, autism rates have skyrocketed; what used to be a very rare and unheard of condition now affects nearly 1 percent of all children. Autism has grave consequences for sufferers and their families. Many cannot have normal relationships, hold jobs, or live without assistance, which is very expensive. As increasing numbers of autistic children grow into autistic adults, Resnik warns that society will not be equipped to handle them. Therefore, she urges organizations and governments to develop more resources to research the causes of autism, effective treatments, and cutting-edge models of care. With hundreds of thousands of children afflicted and more certainly on the way, Resnik says the United States must acknowledge it is in the midst of an autism epidemic that demands its immediate attention. Resnik is cofounder of the Southwest Autism Research & Resource Center in Phoenix, Arizona.

> *"A diagnosis of autism is being made every 20 minutes."*

Denise D. Resnik, "Autism: Helping Our Kids Must Be a Priority," *Arizona Republic,* July 12, 2009. Revised October 9, 2013. Reproduced with permission.

AS YOU READ, CONSIDER THE FOLLOWING QUESTIONS:

1. How often was autism diagnosed in the early 1990s, according to Resnik? How does that compare with the frequency of diagnoses today?
2. How much does lifetime care for an autistic person cost, according to Resnik?
3. What, according to the author, is the unemployment rate for people with autism?

O ur son, Matthew, celebrated his 22nd birthday this summer, and our family celebrated the progress he has worked so hard to make as he courageously and tirelessly wrestles with autism.

While Matt has made substantial advancements over the years, including a high school diploma, he enters adulthood eating just a handful of different foods, sneaking into his parents' bed three to four nights a week, and entertaining himself with toddler-level movies and computer programs.

> **FAST FACT**
>
> According to a 2012 report by the Autism and Developmental Disabilities Monitoring Network, cases of autism in eight-year-old children increased from 1 in 150 kids in 2002 to 1 in 88 kids just six years later.

Time Is Running Out

In these and many other ways, Matt remains a very atypical young man. Still, he has great potential and select, highly advanced skills in math, computer science and as my sous chef. He is without a doubt the hardest-working young man I know and will make someone a proud and productive employee. He has no problem ticking off a long roster of daily chores and activities programmed on his iPad.

After graduation and together with the Southwest Autism Research & Resource Center (SARRC), we helped him start a home bakery business, called SMILE Biscotti (Supporting Matt's Independent Living Enterprise). He works daily on different aspects of the business—shopping, banking, data entry, packaging and his favorite part, baking!

While the prospects for this budding entrepreneur are promising, Matt's daily routines represent many stark contrasts between his development and that of his typical peers. There's so much he just doesn't understand.

In the early years, we thought we'd have so much time to get him on his track. Time to provide him with thousands of hours of therapy. Time for new scientific discoveries. Time for a miracle. . . .

And now, time is running out, not just for Matt but for an entire generation of kids who fueled the statistics that made autism spectrum disorder (ASD) a national public-health crisis.

A Diagnosis Every 20 Minutes

A diagnosis of autism is being made every 20 minutes. The dramatic increase in the incidence, from one in 10,000 in the early 1990s to

These autistic men live in a group home. Society may not be equipped to handle the increasing numbers of autistic children who will grow into autistic adults.

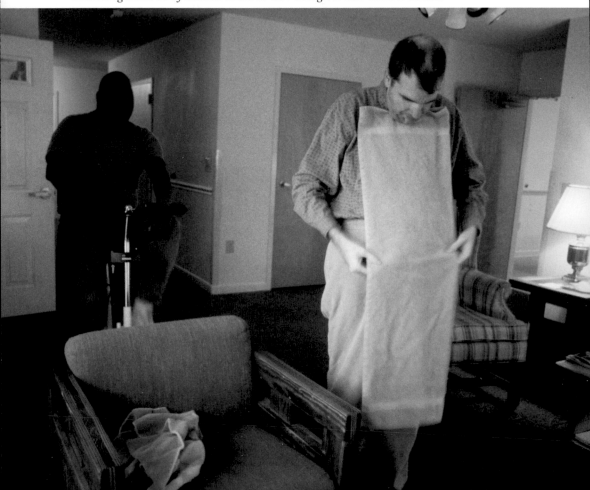

one in 88 today, gives rise to many pressing issues. The cost of caring for an individual with autism throughout his or her lifetime is $3.2 million. The burgeoning population in the U.S. of 1.5 million individuals young and old living with autism is costing our country $125 billon a year.

We know that many adults with autism excel in discrete fields and are great assets to their employers. In fact, some have extraordinary and unique talents that enable them to perform better than their "neurotypical" cohorts. Some individuals with autism excel in positions that involve routine: hard-to-fill, non-customer service jobs in industries such as hospitality, restaurant, hospital, maintenance, data input and data management.

Others excel in jobs that involve systematic, precision work or highly technical support. And many demonstrate lower rates of tardiness, absenteeism and turnover.

But the harsh reality is that even before the Great Recession, unemployment rates for adults with autism hovered around 90 percent, largely a result of their social challenges and lack of training. By comparison, 67 percent of adults with disabilities are unemployed.

The potential of adults with autism to become employed and engaged citizens of the U.S. is not so much limited by their disability but, rather, by the failures of the system charged with supporting them.

A Crisis of This Proportion Demands Attention

To date, there is an absence of federal entitlement legislation intended to support individuals with autism beyond the end of their 21st year, resulting in a confusing web of state-by-state initiatives that often are underfunded and support outdated or inappropriate models of service delivery to a limited number of individuals.

Our country and state urgently need to focus on new models of support and care. We need to design programs that help maximize their independence and engage them in productive daily living. We need accurate information on what constitutes appropriate evidence-based intervention and practice for adults and standards of professional accreditation for direct-care staff.

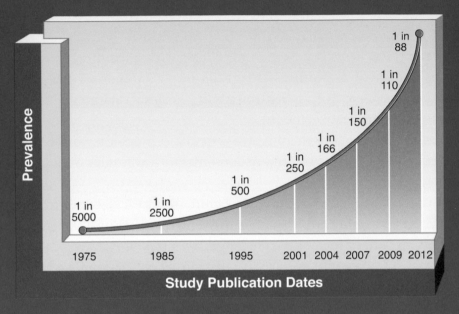

Autism Diagnoses Have Skyrocketed

There has been a more than 600 percent increase in prevalence in autism over the last two decades. As of 2012 about 1 in 88 children had an autism diagnosis, compared with 1 in 5,000 in 1975.

Prevalence

1 in 88

1 in 110

1 in 150

1 in 166

1 in 250

1 in 500

1 in 2500

1 in 5000

1975   1985   1995   2001 2004 2007 2009 2012

Study Publication Dates

Taken from: Autism Speaks, 2009, and the Centers for Disease Control and Prevention, 2012.

We need to reduce the annual turnover rate of caregivers, which exceeds 50 percent, and promote greater professional interest in the provision of quality, effective services and support. We need federal legislation that supports individuals beyond the end of their 21st year and effective strategies for engaging the private sector in solutions.

The time to act is now. With 500,000 children entering adulthood this decade, we can ill afford to wait to achieve consequential action on this challenge as was the case with advancing the agenda for early intervention and insurance coverage.

The Human Costs Are Immeasurable

The Southwest Autism Research & Resource Center (SARRC) and First Place AZ, a new nonprofit dedicated to the housing concerns of adults with autism and related disorders, are currently working with Advancing Futures for Adults with Autism (AFAA), the National Association of Residential Providers for Adults with Autism (NARPAA), Autism Speaks and pioneers across the U.S. to address these and other questions, and create lifelong living opportunities for adults with autism.

SARRC and First Place have been studying existing long-term care options and are advancing models that engage the private sector. We've studied nearly 100 models across the U.S.; identified best practices; and are focused on replicability, scalability and integration of housing within the communities where their families live.

We are breaking ground in 2014 for a new residential prototype empowered by public transit, a suite of amenities and services, and a supportive community in the heart of the city of Phoenix.

We urgently need to consolidate and focus our efforts to develop and drive the agenda for life-long living and learning with autism. Hundreds of thousands of parents of children with autism across the country can no longer afford to wait for answers to the crucial question of who will care for our sons and daughters when we are no longer able to do so. While the economic cost of this system's failure is far reaching, the human cost is immeasurable.

EVALUATING THE AUTHOR'S ARGUMENTS:

Denise D. Resnik, the author of this viewpoint, says that the fact that autism has gone from being a very rare disorder to a very common one proves that America is in the midst of an epidemic. How does Allen Frances, author of the following viewpoint, directly respond to this claim? After reading both viewpoints, with which author do you agree on this point, and why?

America's False Autism Epidemic

Allen Frances

> *"When rates rise this high and this fast, the best bet is always that there has been a change in diagnostic habits, not a real change in people or in the rate of illness."*

America's autism epidemic is false, argues Allen Frances in the following viewpoint. He says the exponential increase in autism rates is not due to an actual increase in the disorder; rather, it is due to a massive overdiagnosis of the condition. He explains that in 1994 the definition of autism was expanded to include conditions that, although serious, should not actually be lumped together with autism. The result, according to Frances, is that every child who has a behavioral, social, learning, or communication disorder receives an autism diagnosis, which dilutes the meaning of autism and exaggerates the extent of the problem. Frances warns that overestimating autism rates does children a grave disservice, especially when it causes their parents to react hysterically to what is in all likelihood an inaccurate assessment of their child's problem. Frances is a professor emeritus at Duke University's department of psychology. He chaired the task force that updated the *Diagnostic and Statistical Manual of Mental Disorders* to its fourth edition, in which the definition of autism was expanded.

AS YOU READ, CONSIDER THE FOLLOWING QUESTIONS:
1. What is Korea's autism rate, according to Frances?
2. What effect does Frances say changing the definition of autism had on the rate of diagnosed cases?
3. What problems are inappropriately lumped under the "tent" of autism, according to Frances?

The apparent epidemic of autism is in fact the latest instance of the fads that litter the history of psychiatry.

We have a strong urge to find labels for disturbing behaviors; naming things gives us an (often false) feeling that we control them. So, time and again, an obscure diagnosis suddenly comes out of nowhere to achieve great popularity. It seems temporarily to explain a lot of previously confusing behavior—but then suddenly and mysteriously returns to obscurity.

Not so long ago, autism was the rarest of diagnoses, occurring in fewer than one in 2,000 people. Now the rate has skyrocketed to 1 in 88 in America (and to a remarkable 1 in 38 in Korea). And there is no end in sight.

Increasingly panicked, parents have become understandably vulnerable to quackery and conspiracy theories. The worst result has been a reluctance to vaccinate kids because of the thoroughly disproved and discredited suggestion that the shots can somehow cause autism.

There are also frantic (and probably futile) efforts to find environmental toxins that might be harming developing brains, explaining the sudden explosion of autism.

Anything is possible, but when rates rise this high and this fast, the best bet is always that there has been a change in diagnostic habits, not a real change in people or in the rate of illness.

So what is really going on to cause this "epidemic"?

Perhaps a third of the huge jump in rates can be explained by three factors: the much-increased public and provider awareness of autism, the much-reduced stigma associated with it and the fact that the definition of autism has been loosened to include milder cases.

Sixteen years ago, when we updated the DSM (the official manual of psych diagnoses) for the fourth edition, we expanded the definition of autism to include Aspergers. At the time, we expected this to triple the rate of diagnosed cases; instead, it has climbed 20 times higher.

That unexpected jump has three obvious causes. Most important, the diagnosis has become closely linked with eligibility for special school services.

Having the label can make the difference between being closely attended to in a class of four versus being lost in a class of 40. Kids who need special attention can often get it only if they are labeled autistic.

Autism Rates by State

Nationally about six students in one thousand are classified as autistic, but the rates vary widely by state. The map of autism rates for children ages six to seventeen shows they are the highest in the Northeast and on the West Coast and lowest among the Southern and Plains states. Some argue that the boom in autism is due not to increased prevalence of the disorder but to widespread overdiagnosis.

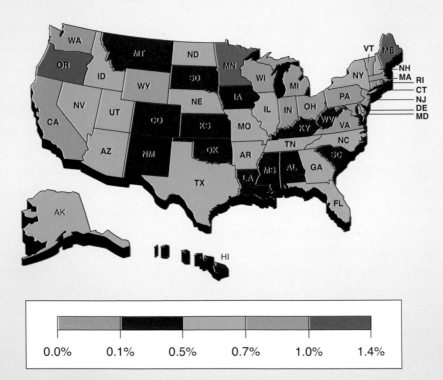

0.0%   0.1%   0.5%   0.7%   1.0%   1.4%

Taken from: Alan Zarembo. "Autism Boom: An Epidemic of Disease or Discovery?" *Los Angeles Times*, December 11, 2011.

So the autism tent has been stretched to accommodate a wide variety of difficult learning, behavioral and social problems that certainly deserve help—but aren't really autism. Probably as many as half of the kids labeled autistic wouldn't really meet the DSM IV criteria if these were applied carefully.

Freeing autism from its too tight coupling with service provision would bring down its rates and end the "epidemic." But that doesn't mean that school services should also be reduced. The mislabeled problems are serious in their own right, and call out for help.

The second driver of the jump in diagnosis has been a remarkably active and successful consumer advocacy on autism, facilitated by the power of the Internet. This has had four big upsides: the identification of previously missed cases, better care and education for the identified cases, greatly expanded research and a huge reduction in stigma.

But there are two unfortunate downsides: Many people with the diagnosis don't really meet the criteria for it, and the diagnosis has become so heterogeneous that it loses meaning and predictive value. This is why so many kids now outgrow their autism. They were never really autistic in the first place.

A third cause has been overstated claims coming from epidemiological research—studies of autism rates in the general population. For reasons of convenience and cost, the ratings in the studies always have to be done by lay interviewers, who aren't trained as clinicians and so are unable to judge whether the elicited symptoms are severe and enduring enough to qualify as a mental disorder.

It's important to understand that the rates reported in these studies are always upper limits, not true rates; they exaggerate the prevalence

Psychiatrist Allen Frances (pictured) says that almost every child who has a behavioral, social, learning, or communication disorder receives an autism diagnosis, which dilutes the meaning of autism and greatly exaggerates the disorder's incidence.

of autism by including people who'd be excluded by careful clinical interview. (This also explains why rates can change so quickly from year to year.)

So where do we stand, and what should we do? I am for a more careful and restricted diagnosis of autism that isn't driven by service requirements. I am also for kids getting the school services they need.

The only way to achieve both goals is to reduce the inordinate power of the diagnosis of autism in determining who gets what educational service. Psychiatric diagnosis is devised for use in clinical settings, not educational ones. It may help contribute to educational decisions but should not determine them.

Human nature changes slowly, if at all, but the ways we label it can change fast and tend to follow fleeting fashions.

EVALUATING THE AUTHOR'S ARGUMENTS:

How do you think the other authors in this chapter would respond to Allen Frances's suggestion that autism is not an epidemic? For each author, write one to two sentences on what their likely response would be. Then state your own opinion on the issue. Should autism be viewed as an epidemic? Why or why not?

The Definition of Autism Should Not Be Narrowed

Laura McKenna

"For those of us whose lives are inextricable from the politics of autism, it is the label— the one that was so difficult for us to accept at first—that has been the key to getting help for our children."

In the following viewpoint Laura McKenna argues that narrowing the definition of autism will deprive children and their families of much needed help. She explains that psychologists are considering making the definition of autism much narrower, so it will be harder to be diagnosed with the condition. The result is that fewer kids will be labeled as autistic, but according to McKenna, this does not mean that they no longer have the disorder. The only thing it will change is that their families, who are already struggling from the emotional, social, and financial demands of raising developmentally challenged children, will need to pay out of pocket for the treatments and services that their children require. McKenna thinks the definition change is an academic exercise in semantics that will have a devastating effect on thousands of families. For these reasons, she thinks it is a mistake to narrow the definition of autism.

Laura McKenna, PhD, is a freelance writer, a former political science professor who writes regularly for *The Atlantic* (the magazine where this viewpoint was originally published), and a parent of a child with an autistic spectrum disorder.

AS YOU READ, CONSIDER THE FOLLOWING QUESTIONS:
1. How does the DSM V (also referred to as DSM-5) definition of autism describe the condition, according to McKenna?
2. Describe what communication skills Ian, the author's son, possessed at two and three years old.
3. What three different kinds of therapies does McKenna say Ian qualified for once he became labeled as autistic?

E veryone, now, has something to say about autism. While TV shows, such as *Touch*, portray autistic children as possessing superhuman powers, the American Psychiatric Association (APA) is busy revising its definition of the disorder to focus on only the most affected individuals. Under their new revision of the Diagnostic and Statistical Manual of Mental Disorders [DSM], the tome that describes and codes psychiatric issues ranging from autism to substance abuse to schizophrenia, people with higher functioning autism, sometimes called PDD or Aspergers or simply high functioning autism, could lose the autistic label.

The New Autism Definition

The new DSM V definition, which reads like a Dim Sum menu of dysfunction, states that an autistic person must have three deficits in social communication, show two out of four patterns of repetitive behavior, and begin to display deficits in childhood. Together, these deficits must impair everyday life. The previous definition in DSM IV had more options on its menu and would include kids whose issues were lumped in one area. The new definition also adds language that would only apply to the most severely affected individuals. It's no longer just about showing an "apparently inflexible adherence to specific, nonfunctional routines or rituals."

What's in a name? Why is the autism community up in arms about this change in the DSM? What exactly is at stake?

Ian's Story

When my son turned two, he could not talk. He made hand gestures to ask for things, but the words that swam around in his head could not come out of his mouth. To make sense of the world, he taught himself to read. At three, when he was upset, we would write him notes, instead of talking to him. He understood written words better than anything we said to him.

Ian was clearly different than other kids. In very important ways, he was disabled. In less important ways, he was gifted. What was wrong with him?

When my son stopped developing like other kids, I took him to see specialists. Because he didn't look classically autistic, they gave him a dozen other labels for his condition—Sensory Integration Disorder, Apraxia, Speech Delay. He didn't receive an autism diagnosis from a neurologist until he was five. The doctor sat us down in the examining room and asked, "has anyone ever used the word autism with you?" We sat in stunned silence in that room for 20 minutes trying to wrap our minds around this word.

> **FAST FACT**
>
> According to a June 2012 Autistic Self Advocacy Network policy brief, 419,262 students aged three to twenty-one receive special education services under the Individuals with Disabilities Education Act. Changing the definition of autism may reclassify many of those students, making them ineligible for special education.

"The Autism Label Was Our Savior"

After we recovered from that blow, we slowly realized that the autism label was our savior. Ian now qualified for a school that specialized in high functioning autistic kids. There, he received targeted help from individuals with an expertise in autism. He received speech therapy four times a week, occupational therapy to help with his fine motor control, and ABA [applied behavior analysis] therapy to help him con-

The Diagnostic and Statistical Manual of Mental Disorders *describes and codes psychiatric dianoses ranging from autism to substance abuse to schizophrenia. New classifications of autism have narrowed its definition.*

trol his focus and limit his OCD [obsessive-compulsive disorder] tics. While our insurance company still tortured us about paying for certain therapies, laws were in place that gave us some protections. In the state of New Jersey, the Autism Insurance Act requires that private insurance cover diagnosis and many programs for the autistic. With his new schools and services, Ian made rapid progress.

During those three years when we wandered lost through the forest of disability labels, Ian missed out on years of services that would have better targeted his needs. I suppose that regret is an inevitable part of parenthood. For us, we'll always regret that we didn't find the right label for him until later.

Do Not Take Away Our Passport to Help

According to the APA's new definition, autistic children should have "excessive adherence" to routines and have "highly restricted" interests. Those words, excessive and highly, are subjective and might exclude my son, as well as all of his classmates. Outside the school, as they wait to pick up their kids, the nervous parents whisper. If our children no longer qualify as autistic, what will happen to them? Will insurance companies pay for their speech and ABA therapy? Will the school district pull them out of their special classrooms? So many parents of autistic children have huge financial problems due to unreimbursed therapy and the loss of income. Will this new law make their financial burden worse?

Make no mistake: What may appear to be a purely academic debate over the autism label will have a real impact on thousands of families. For those of us whose lives are inextricable from the politics of autism, it is the label—the one that was so difficult for us to accept at first—that has been the key to getting help for our children.

EVALUATING THE AUTHOR'S ARGUMENTS:

This viewpoint's author, Laura McKenna, has a child with autism and believes that narrowing its definition will hurt autistic people, while the author of the previous viewpoint, Allen Frances, is a psychiatrist who helped revise the *Diagnostic and Statistical Manual of Mental Disorders-IV*, which expanded the definition of autism but warns about overdiagnosing the disorder based on the expanded definition. What are some of the drawbacks of overdiagnosing autism, in each author's opinion?

Catastrophic Autism Rate Now 1 in 88, 1 in 54 Boys; Advocacy Groups Ask What Will It Take for the Feds to Act?

"Secretary Sebelius should declare [autism] a national health emergency."

PRWeb

PRWeb is an online news distribution and online publicity organization. In the following viewpoint the author reports on a press conference of autism support organizations. The representatives declare that the number of autism cases has reached epidemic proportions and that the federal government should declare autism an epidemic and investigate past funding and health agency failures.

AS YOU READ, CONSIDER THE FOLLOWING QUESTIONS:
1. As reported by the author, what age group has one in eighty-eight children with autism?
2. According to the author, recent research from Stanford University conclusively shows that what triggers autism?
3. According to the article, most of the funding for autism research has been spent on what?

*N*ew York, NY (PRWEB) March 30, 2012—The Focus Autism Foundation joins a coalition of autism groups in a press conference on World Autism Day, blast HHS ongoing failures.

Grassroots autism advocacy organizations representing over 100,000 autism families will hold a press conference Monday, April 2, 2012, World Autism Day, at 11:00 at Hilton Manhattan East, 304 East 42nd St., to push for official recognition of autism as a national public health emergency and to analyze the federal health authorities' ongoing failure to respond.

Yesterday the Centers for Disease Control and Prevention announced new prevalence rates among 8-year-olds from 2008 as 1 in 88 children and 1 in 54 boys. "These numbers are staggering," said Katie Wright, daughter of Autism Speaks co-founders Bob and Suzanne Wright and board member of the National Autism Association and of Focus Autism. "When will the federal health authorities wake up? Will it be 1 in 25? 1 in 10? How many children have to suffer from autism to call this an emergency?"

Recent research from Stanford University conclusively shows that environmental triggers account for most cases of autism, not genetic predisposition. "Parents have been calling on the NIH to study environmental factors for decades, but almost all the money has gone into genetic studies. No matter how high the autism rate soars, the CDC's

> **FAST FACT**
>
> A poll conducted by the National Alliance for Autism Research found that 89 percent of Americans support increasing research funding for autism.

continued denial of an autism epidemic is a certitude comparable to death and taxes," said Mark Blaxill, Editor-at-Large of Age of Autism web-based newspaper.

These advocacy groups believe that ongoing government research appears to be driven by corporations that fear being implicated in any environmental relationship with the autism epidemic, and believe that these apparent conflicts of interest must be exposed.

The organizations call for three urgent action steps:

1. Secretary Sebelius should declare a national health emergency and order the NIH and CDC to shift their research focus to prevention efforts, especially investigation of long overlooked environmental factors.
2. The Government Accounting Office should initiate a study of past research funding that has ignored environmental causes. We need to understand whether this was the result of lobbying to avoid possible liability that might be uncovered with examination of environmental triggers.
3. The U.S. House of Representatives Government Reform Committee should initiate promised hearings as soon as possible on the failure of federal health agencies in appropriately responding to this epidemic. It has been about ten years since this Committee examined the role of the federal authorities in the

Autism advocates, such as Katie Wright, daughter of Autism Speaks founders and board member of the National Autism Association, met for a press conference to declare that the autism problem has become an epidemic and the federal government should declare autism a national health emergency and focus research efforts on prevention.

Americans Support Government Funding for Autism Research

89%

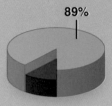

support increasing research funding for autism.

53%

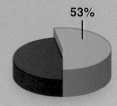

think autism does not receive enough funding from the federal government.

64%

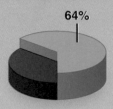

think there should be more federal funding for autism research.

Taken from: National Alliance for Autism Research.

autism epidemic. We can think of no other instance of any comparable epidemic that has gone on so long without Congressional oversight.

Grassroots organizations represented at the press conference: Age of Autism, AutismOne, Autism Action Network, Autism File, The Canary Party, Center for Personal Rights, The Coalition for Safe Minds, Elizabeth Birt Center for Autism Law and Advocacy, Focus Autism, National Autism Association, Talk About Curing Autism Press conference:

Monday, April 2 11:00 a.m.
Hilton Manhattan East
304 East 42nd St.

EVALUATING THE AUTHOR'S ARGUMENTS:

The author, PRWeb, reports on the press conference held by autism support groups on World Autism Day 2012. What parts of the support group's arguments do you find the most convincing? The least convincing? Why?

The Autism-Welfare Nexus

Paul Sperry

In the following viewpoint Paul Sperry argues that the federal government should not respond to what he says is an exaggerated autism epidemic. In his opinion, the phenomenal increase in autism cases over the past two decades is the result of overdiagnosis and an overly broad definition of autism, not new cases of the disorder. Yet belief in an epidemic has spawned numerous expensive federal programs that waste money and resources, says Sperry. He accuses the country's leaders of using autism hysteria to grow the federal government and offer services and benefits to families who do not really need it. He warns that as more people accept funding for services that stretch into adulthood, a welfare state springs up around the autism industry, which he says is making doctors, pharmaceutical companies, and other kinds of service providers rich. Sperry says the nation must get over its autism obsession and not allow billions of federal dollars to be wasted on services for kids who are simply emotional, have behavioral problems, or are just a little different. Sperry is an editorial writer for the *Investor's Business Daily*, where this viewpoint was originally published.

> "The [Barack] Obama administration is exploiting the 'epidemic' to increase the size of the federal government."

AS YOU READ, CONSIDER THE FOLLOWING QUESTIONS:
1. Who is Steve Jobs and how does he factor into the author's argument?
2. Explain the autism benefits package as laid out by Health and Human Services Secretary Kathleen Sebelius.
3. According to Sperry, how many children were on federal disability for autism as of December 2010?

I f Steve Jobs were a child today, his school no doubt would drag his parents into the office and tell them he was so difficult and disruptive he needed to be examined by a doctor.

His chastened parents, in turn, would take him to a pediatrician who more than likely would diagnose him with high-functioning autism and prescribe a daily regimen of Prozac or Ritalin.

Prescriptions in hand, his working-class parents could then apply for federal disability benefits. And his school could qualify for more federal aid.

Duly medicated and labeled "disabled," Jobs probably would never grow up to invent cutting-edge technologies or revolutionize industries.

This is the Orwellian world in which we live today in the age of autism hysteria. And it will only get worse, thanks to ObamaCare.

In honor of April's National Autism Awareness Month, Health and Human Services Secretary Kathleen Sebelius laid out ObamaCare's new autism benefits package.

"Under the new health care law, insurers will no longer be allowed to deny children coverage for Autism Spectrum Disorder or other pre-existing conditions; lifetime dollar limits on coverage are prohibited; new plans must cover autism screening at no additional cost to parents; and young adults without employer-provided insurance may remain on their parents' health insurance until they turn 26," she announced, just four days after naming her new autism advisory board, which includes every key player in the growing autism lobby.

This powerful lobby is feeding the hysteria and creating an appetite for greater federal funding. And the Obama administration is exploiting the "epidemic" to increase the size of the federal government.

"Also," Sebelius said, "starting in 2014, individuals with Autism Spectrum Disorder will have expanded access to affordable insurance options through new affordable insurance exchanges and Medicaid."

A week before the health commissar made it easier to diagnose and medicate kids for the disorder, the Federal Centers For Disease Control officially declared it an epidemic. In late March, CDC claimed 1 in 88 kids now has autism, up 78% from 2000.

But buried in its report is a disclaimer noting that the number of cases may be inflated due to "the change to a broader, more inclusive definition" of autism.

Few caveats are more understated.

In 1994, medical officials and the Clinton administration broadened the definition to include children who previously might have been thought of as odd.

Today milder conditions, such as speech impediments and extreme shyness, are covered in addition to severe autism under the new umbrella: Autism Spectrum Disorder.

Before the 1990s, when only 1 in 2,500 were diagnosed as autistic, symptoms were obvious. Kids with classic autism didn't speak or make eye contact. They hit themselves. They soiled themselves.

Many even ate broken glass.

Now more than half of autism cases fall under the mildest range of the spectrum, known as Asperger's disorder. These kids fidget. Or brood. Or they may pick their nose and eat only yellow foods. But they are high-functioning students who will be able to hold jobs as adults.

And they shouldn't be labeled mentally disabled.

There Is No Epidemic

A growing body of scientific research has found that the rise in autism diagnoses is not due to a true increase in the incidence of the cognitive disorder, but rather to a widening of the definition and increased screening by schools and doctors, who are rushing to diagnose and medicate socially awkward or difficult kids.

According to recent studies that control for changes in the diagnostic criteria, the rate of autism has actually been stable over time.

And the number of language disorder cases have fallen as autism cases have risen, suggesting one disorder has simply been substituted for another.

In other words, there is no autism epidemic. The problem is mostly statistical.

Yet President Obama has pledged $1 billion for autism research that includes studying alleged "environmental factors" leading to the "epidemic."

That's on top of the hundreds of millions in new spending on special education and disability benefits for autism.

The number of children receiving such benefits has surged since the 1990s, when the Clinton administration expanded coverage to include the mental disorder.

Now autism is the fastest-growing category within the Supplemental Security Income program, which was intended to serve kids with congenital and physical disabilities like cerebral palsy and Down syndrome.

As of December 2010, the latest Social Security Administration data show, almost 100,000 children were on federal disability for autism. Parents filed 23,203 new applications in 2010, quadrupling 2000's total of 5,430.

> ## FAST FACT
>
> A 2006 study by the Harvard School of Public Health estimated that it costs about $3.2 million to care for an individual with autism over his or her lifetime and that it costs about $35 billion per year to care for all of society's autistic individuals.

Officials rarely review autism cases, making the program—which pays up to $700 in monthly cash benefits with no spending restrictions—vulnerable to fraud and abuse.

In fact, it's evolving into yet another welfare boondoggle. Many high-functioning teens are discouraged from working for fear of losing their disability status and benefits, which will only create a cycle of government dependency and poverty.

Health and social workers coach parents applying for benefits to obtain a prescription for autism medication, since kids on meds are more likely to be approved (other tips include listing bad "personal hygiene" as a symptom).

Also in the 1990s, Washington added autism as a separate disability category to a federal law guaranteeing special education services at public expense.

Insurance Coverage for Autism

At least thirty-two states specifically require insurers to provide coverage for either diagnosis and/or treatment of autism spectrum disorders. Some argue that families desperately need this coverage, as it can cost as much as fifty thousand dollars per year to care for an autistic child. Others argue that autism is wildly overdiagnosed and the billions of dollars in subsidies for treatments are unnecessary and inappropriate.

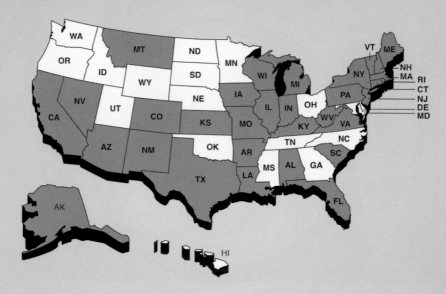

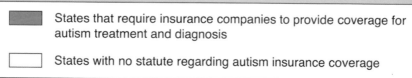

States that require insurance companies to provide coverage for autism treatment and diagnosis

States with no statute regarding autism insurance coverage

Towering Achievements

This, in turn, has led to a surge in special ed funding for schools. There's now a powerful incentive for administrators to increase their autism head counts.

Autism also is big business for doctors and drugmakers. And now, HHS and CDC are working with the Academy of American Pediatrics

Health and Human Services secretary Kathleen Sebelius (pictured) issued a statement on National Autism Awareness Month promoting the benefits of the new Afforable Care Act for people with autism. She stated that "because of the health care law, insurers are not allowed to exclude children with autism based on their pre-existing condition."

to recommend doctors screen children at a much younger age—starting at 18 months and then again at 24 months.

There's no blood test for autism. Diagnoses are based strictly on observation. So watch the caseload soar even higher.

And watch the autism industry grow bigger. All told, it already costs the U.S. about $35 billion each year to care for people with autism.

Hans Asperger, the doctor who originally observed kids with what he called high-functioning autism, wrote that their narrowly focused interests can drive them to achieve things that are impossible for normal people.

It was said of Jobs—the socially awkward loner prone to angry outbursts, who grew up to found the world's largest company—that whatever he was interested in he would generally carry it to an "irrational extreme."

Thank goodness.

The American Psychiatric Association is completing its first major revision to its diagnostic manual since 1995, when cases first took off.

Let's hope it corrects its error and narrows the definition back to classic autism before this false epidemic and welfare lobby grow any bigger.

EVALUATING THE AUTHOR'S ARGUMENTS:

In this viewpoint Paul Sperry is cynical about the problem of autism—he warns that a welfare state is growing around the chronic overdiagnosis of autism and that many sectors of society profit from the disorder. Do you agree with his characterization of the problem? Why or why not? Quote from the texts you have read to support your answer.

Chapter 3

How Can Autism Be Reduced, Treated, or Cured?

Controversy abounds over what methods should be used to treat autism.

Gluten-Free, Casein-Free Diet More Effective in Improving ASD Behaviors and Symptoms

Penn State

> *"Our findings suggest that a gluten-free, casein-free diet might be beneficial for some children on the autism spectrum."*

Pennsylvania State University (Penn State) is a major public research university, where the research mentioned here was conducted and then reported in News-Medical.Net, a medical-information provider. In the following viewpoint the author reports on survey data from 387 caregivers of children with autism who have kept their children on a gluten- and casein-free diet. The data suggest that physiological and sociological symptoms of autistic children improved with strict adherence to the diet.

Penn State, "Gluten-Free, Casein-Free Diet More Effective in Improving ASD Behaviors and Symptoms," News-Medical.Net, March 1, 2012. Reproduced with permission.

AS YOU READ, CONSIDER THE FOLLOWING QUESTIONS:
1. According to the viewpoint, social behaviors improved by the gluten- and casein-free diet include what?
2. According to Klein, one of the researchers, how does the gluten-free/casein-free diet affect pain receptors, the immune system, and the brain?
3. According to the article, gluten and casein were examined because they possess what characteristic?

Agluten-free, casein-free diet may lead to improvements in behavior and physiological symptoms in some children diagnosed with an autism spectrum disorder (ASD), according to researchers at Penn State. The research is the first to use survey data from parents to document the effectiveness of a gluten-free, casein-free diet on children with ASD.

"Research has shown that children with ASD commonly have GI [gastrointestinal] symptoms," said Christine Pennesi, medical student at Penn State College of Medicine. "Notably, a greater proportion of our study population reported GI and allergy symptoms than what is seen in the general pediatric population. Some experts have suggested that gluten- and casein-derived peptides cause an immune response in children with ASD, and others have proposed that the peptides could trigger GI symptoms and behavioral problems."

The team—which included Laura Cousino Klein, associate professor of biobehavioral health and human development and family studies—asked 387 parents or primary caregivers of children with ASD to complete a 90-item online survey about their children's GI symptoms, food allergy diagnoses, and suspected food sensitivities, as well as their children's degree of adherence to a gluten-free, casein-free diet. The team's results appeared online this month in the journal *Nutritional Neuroscience*.

Pennesi and Klein and their team found that a gluten-free, casein-free diet was more effective in improving ASD behaviors, physiological symptoms and social behaviors for those children with GI symptoms and with allergy symptoms compared to those without these symptoms. Specifically, parents noted improved GI symptoms in their children as well as increases in their children's social behaviors, such as language production, eye contact, engagement, attention span, requesting behavior and social responsiveness, when they strictly followed a gluten-free, casein-free diet.

According to Klein, autism may be more than a neurological disease—it may involve the GI tract and the immune system.

The author claims that a diet free of gluten, which is found in foods made with (clockwise from top left) barley, wheat, rye, and oats, and casein, a protein found in dairy products, can alleviate symptoms of autism.

A study undertaken by the Interactive Autism Network polled parents who tried their autistic children on special diets, including the gluten-free/casein–free diet. The majority reported seeing moderate, high, or very high levels of improvement in their children.

GF/CF Diet—Level of Improvement
Ratings by Parents of Children with Autism Spectrum Disorders (ASD)

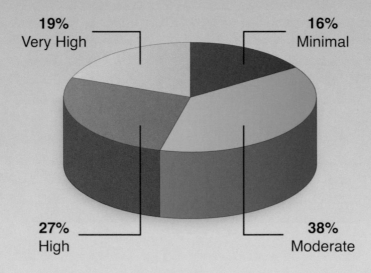

19%
Very High

16%
Minimal

27%
High

38%
Moderate

Taken from: Interactive Autism Network. "IAN Research Findings: Special Diets," November 11, 2008.

"There are strong connections between the immune system and the brain, which are mediated through multiple physiological symptoms," Klein said. "A majority of the pain receptors in the body are located in the gut, so by adhering to a gluten-free, casein-free diet, you're reducing inflammation and discomfort that may alter brain processing, making the body more receptive to ASD therapies."

The team found that parents who eliminated all gluten and casein from their children's diets reported that a greater number of their children's ASD behaviors, physiological symptoms and social behaviors improved after starting the diet compared to children whose parents did not eliminate all gluten and casein. The team also found that parents who implemented the diet for six months or less reported that the diet was less effective in reducing their child's ASD behaviors.

According to the researchers, some of the parents who filled out the surveys had eliminated only gluten or only casein from their children's diets, but survey results suggested that parents who completely eliminated both gluten and casein from their child's diet reported the most benefit.

"While more rigorous research is needed, our findings suggest that a gluten-free, casein-free diet might be beneficial for some children on the autism spectrum," Pennesi said. "It is also possible that there are other proteins, such as soy, that are problematic for these children."

FAST FACT

According to a study by the autism advocacy organization Autism Speaks, nearly half of all children with autism experience gastrointestinal symptoms.

The reason Klein and Pennesi examined gluten and casein is because they are two of the most common "diet offenders."

"Gluten and casein seem to be the most immunoreactive," Klein said. "A child's skin and blood tests for gluten and casein allergies can be negative, but the child still can have a localized immune response in the gut that can lead to behavioral and psychological symptoms. When you add that in with autism you can get an exacerbation of effects."

Klein's advice to parents of children with ASD?

"If parents are going to try a gluten-free, casein-free diet with their children, they really need to stick to it in order to receive the possible benefits," she said.

"It might give parents an opportunity to talk with their physicians about starting a gluten-free, casein-free diet with their children with ASD."

This viewpoint reports on a survey conducted by research-ers at Penn State University that suggests that a gluten-free/casein-free diet could improve symptoms in children with ASD. What do you think the researchers would say to the criticisms of the diet expressed by the author of the fol-lowing viewpoint?

A Gluten-Free/ Casein-Free Diet Does Not Cure Autism

Dan Childs, Lara Salahi, and Pamela Mazzeo

"I have had many families who have tried GFCF diets and have not found a real difference in their children's behaviors."

Dan Childs, Lara Salahi, and Pamela Mazzeo are reporters for ABC News. In the following viewpoint they report on a study that found no significant benefits from reducing or eliminating gluten and casein from an autistic child's diet. For one month, researchers gave one group of autistic children foods that contained gluten and casein, and another group foods that did not. They found no significant differences in the children's behavior, ability to pay attention, or whether they displayed other symptoms associated with autism. Researchers concluded that although the gluten-free/casein-free (GF/CF) diet is popular, there is no scientific evidence to prove it actually works. The researchers suggest that autistic children are likely better served by behavioral therapies than by diets.

Dan Childs, Lara Salahi, and Pamela Mazzeo, "Gluten-Free, Casein-Free Diet No Remedy for Autism," *ABC News,* May 19, 2010. Reproduced with permission.

A popular diet intended to curb the effects of autism received yet another blow today in the form of a new study that found that autistic children who adhered to a gluten-free, casein-free [GFCF] diet showed no improvement in their symptoms.

Gluten is a protein found in wheat, and casein is a protein found in dairy products.

No Significant Benefits

Dr. Susan Hyman, lead author of the study, said she knows that some families would be surprised by the team's findings, especially given the reports of dramatic clinical improvement observed by many families using the diet.

"It would have been wonderful for children with autism and their families if we found that the GFCF diet could really help, but this small study didn't show significant benefits," Hyman, an associate professor of pediatrics at Golisano Children's Hospital at the University of Rochester Medical Center, said in a statement. But she did say it was possible that children with significant gastrointestinal disease would reap some benefits from the diet.

Still, Tracey McCollum, the mother of one of the children in the study, said the results were personally disheartening.

"We were hoping to show that the diet made a difference, give a lot of parents some hopes that, 'Here's a magic bullet; here is something that I can do proactively that will help my child," she said. "As a parent you want to do everything you can to help your child do the best he can in life."

The study will be presented May 22 [2010] at the International Meeting for Autism Research in Philadelphia.

Disappointing Findings

The researchers undertook a randomized, double-blinded (meaning neither the participants nor the researchers knew which treatment anyone received), placebo-controlled study.

Fourteen children who were put on the diet for at least four weeks were then given snacks containing gluten, casein, both or neither. The researchers evaluated the children for changes in attention, sleep, stool [bowel movement] patterns and characteristic autistic behavior. The study did not show significant changes in any of these symptoms for any of the groups.

Dr. Leonard Rappaport, chief of the Division of Developmental Medicine at Children's Hospital in Boston, called the findings "disappointing."

"Even though I did not believe it really made a difference, I was hoping I was wrong," Rappaport said.

GF/CF Offers Little Help Against Autism

Dr. Ari Brown, a pediatrician and author of the books "Expecting 411," "Baby 411" and "Toddler 411," said that though she believes the study is "far from definitive," the results were not unanticipated.

"I have had many families who have tried GFCF diets and have not found a real difference in their children's behaviors," she said. "I do have a few who claim it does help, but those children also are involved in some behavioral therapy, so it is hard to tease out which treatment has been beneficial."

But David Amaral, president of the International Society for Autism Research and professor at the University of California at Davis, said that the findings may not necessarily be cause for dismay among parents of autistic children.

"Actually, I don't think that many parents will be disappointed," Amaral said. "On the contrary, it is very difficult to maintain children on the [GFCF] diet. Some parents who may have failed in maintaining the diet may feel relieved to hear that it might not be a benefit to their child even if they had persisted."

A Popular Diet, but Scientifically Unproven

Many parents of autistic children look to alternative therapies, including special diets. According to Dr. Daniel Coury, medical director of

The GF/CF Burden

Parents go to extreme lengths—including quitting their job and spending hundreds of dollars a month—to put their autistic children on a gluten-free/casein-free diet. Some question whether this is wise, considering a lack of scientific evidence proving it works.

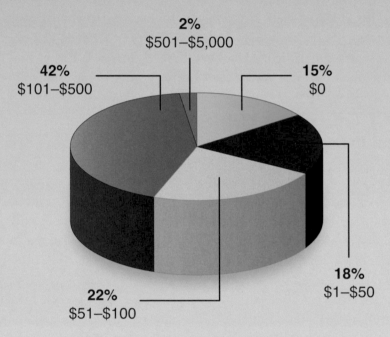

The GF/CF Diet
Reported Cost per Month

2%
$501–$5,000

42%
$101–$500

15%
$0

18%
$1–$50

22%
$51–$100

Taken from: Interactive Autism Network. "IAN Research Findings: Special Diets," November 11, 2008.

the Autism Treatment Network, about 20 percent of parents within the network use complementary methods to treat their autistic children, and more than half of them rely to some extent on diets.

In particular, parents of autistic children often report improvements with the popular but scientifically unproven gluten-free, casein-free diet.

This diet has been promoted by celebrities such as Jenny McCarthy, whose best-selling book, "Louder Than Words," detailed her use of diets as one way of treating her autistic son. Many autism communities have also touted the purported benefits of specialized diets for their children.

While many parents of children with autism report gastrointestinal pain in their children, the question remains whether the association between autism and bowel disease exists.

Diets Do Not Help

Not all parents have had success with the diets. Diane Marshall, 42, of Montclair, N.J., put her son David, 13, on a gluten-free, casein-free diet for a year when he was 4 years old. Marshall said she'd read success stories from some mothers who tried the diet for their autistic children. At the time, David had severe eczema and runny bowel movements, she said.

"We definitely thought the diet would help the autism," said Marshall.

Although the gastrointestinal issues subsided, Marshall said she did not attribute the end of her son's stomach problems to the diet. And she said the diet did not help her son overcome autism.

"There are a lot of things out there that are based on evidence, like teaching methods, that will help our kids a lot, but not diets," said Marshall.

"There has not been any research to substantiate the GFCF diet for children with autism who do not have celiac disease or wheat/milk allergies," said Dr. Stefani Hines, a development-behavioral pediatrician at William Beaumont children's hospital in Royal Oak, Mich.

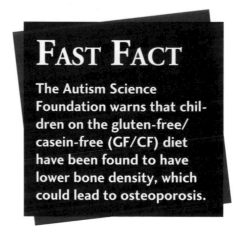

FAST FACT

The Autism Science Foundation warns that children on the gluten-free/casein-free (GF/CF) diet have been found to have lower bone density, which could lead to osteoporosis.

Behavioral Therapies More Effective

But this does not mean that parents are necessarily empty-handed when it comes to scientific approaches to improving autism symptoms, Hines said.

A child finishes a gluten-free breakfast. The authors cite a study that found no significant benefits from reducing or eliminating gluten and casein from an autistic child's diet.

"So far the research that has been the most promising has been aimed at applied behavioral analysis," she said. "We still have much to learn regarding best treatment practices for children with autism."

Study author Hyman said more research needs to be done in this area with similar rigor but with larger numbers, so that subtle effects can be detected. It's important, she said, for families to get the best information they can in deciding which interventions to pursue.

She also said families who elect to make dietary changes need to pay careful attention to general nutrition. "When you eliminate dairy as an entire category, you need to pay attention to vitamin D, calcium and protein," she said.

Rappaport agreed. "I hope that parents will go into these diets with their eyes open—using a nutritionist to guide them—and even if there seems to be anecdotal improvement, that they try the child off this restrictive diet after a while to see if it actually makes a difference."

Parents Are Desperate

In the meantime, Hines said doctors should not be surprised if parents continue to use the diet to try to improve autism symptoms in their children, despite the weight of the research.

"Autism is a chronic, lifelong condition with no known cure," Hines said. "Parents will continue to try everything out there to make sure they aren't missing anything that could possibly help their child.

"Our job as care providers is to help them along in this process and to try to wade through all the data with them to make the best-informed decisions."

EVALUATING THE AUTHOR'S ARGUMENTS:

This viewpoint presents results of a study that shows a gluten-free/casein-free diet has no significant benefits for autistic children. In the previous viewpoint, however, research performed at Penn State claims the GF/CF diet has helped many autistic children. How do you account for these discrepancies? How might you explain these two groups' differences of opinion on this matter?

Reducing Pesticide Exposure Could Reduce Autism

"Exposures to pesticides during fetal development, infancy and childhood may contribute significantly to [a] decline in the cognitive abilities of our children."

**Pesticide Action Network
North America**

The following viewpoint was published by Pesticide Action Network North America (PANNA), a group that researches hazardous pesticide use and seeks to replace it with ecologically sound and safe alternatives. The group argues that reducing pesticide exposure could reduce the skyrocketing cases of autism and other neurobehavioral disorders. PANNA explains how pesticides and other commonly used chemicals affect brain development in fetuses and children, causing damage that results in the symptoms of autism and other disorders. The group claims that a sizable portion of all autism cases can be attributed either to direct pesticide exposure or to the unique way in which pesticides interact with certain people's genetic predispositions. PANNA urges lawmakers and families to become more aware of the presence of pesticides in their homes and communities and to protect the developing minds of children from these chemicals.

AS YOU READ, CONSIDER THE FOLLOWING QUESTIONS:
1. What portion of all neurobehavioral disorders does the author report are caused either directly by pesticides or by the interaction between chemicals and genetics?
2. What were the results of a study that focused on sprayed fields in California's Central Valley?
3. What did a study of infants in New York City find about the link between the chemical chlorpyrifos and autism?

The process of establishing the architecture of the human brain begins in the womb and continues into early adulthood. During this long window of development, many complex processes take place, involving tens of billions of nerve cells making trillions of connections. Cells migrate from one section of the brain to another, and nerve tracts are laid as the final structure of the brain is created.

Many of the processes that occur during brain development are vulnerable to disruption from pesticides. Exposure to neurotoxic pesticides during critical moments of fetal development, even at very low levels, has been shown to fundamentally alter brain architecture. Pesticides that disrupt the hormone system—and [in] particular those affecting the functioning of the thyroid, which plays a key role in brain development—can cause lasting damage. The impacts of exposures are often irreversible because unlike other organs, the brain cannot repair damaged cells.

Children whose brain infrastructure or nervous system fails to develop normally may be disabled for the rest of their lives. Developmental disabilities include autism spectrum disorders, attention deficit disorders, hearing loss, intellectual impairment and vision loss. People with developmental disabilities are often challenged by everyday life activities such as language, mobility, learning and independent living. Reduced cognitive abilities can also lead to behavioral problems, from aggression and social alienation to increased risk of drug abuse.

A "Silent Pandemic"

Some 15 percent of all U.S. children have one or more developmental disabilities—representing a 17 percent increase in the past decade. For some disorders, the numbers are rising even more rapidly. Overall, researchers estimate that between 400,000 and 600,000 of the four million U.S. children born each year are affected by a neurodevelopmental disorder.

Public health experts from Harvard and Mt. Sinai Hospital have called the damage that chemicals are causing children's developing minds a "silent pandemic," and scientists now point to a combination of genetic and environmental factors to explain this rapid rise of developmental, learning and behavioral disabilities.

Some children, for example, may have a genetic susceptibility to attention deficit/hyperactivity disorder (ADHD) or autism, but it may only develop if the child is exposed to a triggering chemical during a certain period of development. Other children may be genetically programmed to produce less of a common detoxifying enzyme, rendering their brain and nervous system more susceptible to lasting harm when they are exposed to neurotoxic pesticides.

Genetic mutations that occur in parents (both men and women) in response to chemical exposures over the course of their lifetime can also, according to recent research, raise the risk of neurodevelopmental disorders for their children.

Pesticide Exposure Wreaks Havoc

The National Academy of Sciences now estimates that about one third of all neurobehavioral disorders (such as autism and ADHD) are caused either directly by pesticides and other chemicals or by interaction between environmental exposures and genetics. Some experts say this estimate is likely to be low, as the health profession is just beginning to fully recognize the contributions of environmental factors to disease formation.

Whatever the mechanism of harm, recent studies leave little doubt that exposures to pesticides during fetal development, infancy and childhood may contribute significantly to [a] decline in the cognitive abilities of our children. A recent comprehensive review of the science on health effects of pesticides by the Ontario College of Family

The National Academy of Sciences now estimates that about one-third of all neurobehavioral disorders (such as autism and ADHD) are caused either directly by pesticides and other environmental chemicals or by these chemicals' triggering of a genetic response.

Physicians found exposure to pesticides in the womb to be "consistently associated with measurable deficits in child neurodevelopment."...

The Alarming Rise in Autistic Children

The autism spectrum includes classic autism, Asperger's Syndrome and atypical autism. Incidence rates have risen rapidly in recent years; in its 2012 report, CDC [Centers for Disease Control and Prevention] estimated—based on 2008 data on eight-year-olds from

14 states—that 1.1 percent of U.S. children, or one in every 88, are now on the autism spectrum. Boys are more likely to have the disorder, with one in 54 affected.

Data from the National Health Interview Surveys reveal a dramatic rate of increase. Between 1997 and 2008, autism prevalence among boys ages three to 17 years increased 261%. Prevalence among girls, while much lower than boys overall, rose even more quickly, showing an increase of more than 385% over the same period.

In California, the number of children with autism who are enrolled in statewide programs rose from 3,864 in 1987 to 11,995 in 1998, an increase of more than 210 percent in 11 years. Other states saw similar rates of increase between 2002 and 2006. Though shifts in diagnosis account for some of this dramatic rise, public health experts have determined that diagnostic changes do not fully explain the trend.

The Role Chemicals Play

Researchers believe autism spectrum disorders reflect changes in brain structure occurring during critical windows of development in the womb. These shifts in brain architecture may be caused by genetics, environmental insults such as chemical exposure, or an interaction between the two.

In 2012, a group of researchers led by Dr. Philip Landrigan of Mt. Sinai Medical Center released a list of ten types of chemicals most likely to be linked to the development of autism, and laid out an urgent strategy for research into the role of these contaminants and how children can be better protected from them. The list includes both commonly used organophosphate pesticides and longlasting organochlorine pesticides, as well as other chemicals commonly found in consumer products.

Studies examining the links between pesticide exposure and autism suggest prenatal exposures are particularly damaging.

- One study in California's Central Valley [the main agricultural region of the state and a major supplier of US food] found that when mothers were exposed early in pregnancy to the organochlorine pesticides endosulfan and dicofol, the risk of autism among their children increased sharply. Children whose mothers lived within 500 feet of fields being sprayed were six times more likely to be on the autism spectrum.

- Mothers in California's central coast region who had higher levels of organophosphate metabolites in their urine during pregnancy were much more likely to have children with pervasive developmental disorder—which can include or be an indicator of autism. The risk more than doubled each time metabolite concentrations went up by a factor of 10.

- A study in New York City found that infants most exposed to chlorpyrifos *in utero* were significantly more likely to have pervasive developmental disorders—including autism—by the time they were three years old.

- A trio of U.S. studies examined links between environmental exposures among parents (including, but not limited to, pesticides) and incidence of autism among their children. Among other findings, the scientists reported that older fathers are more likely to transmit tiny, spontaneous gene mutations—that occur over a lifetime in response to environmental stressors—to their offspring, that in turn increase the risk of autism. Recent research in Iceland confirmed these findings.

- Minnesota researchers explored the interaction of exposure to organophosphate pesticides, gene expression and dietary factors as potential contributors to autism. Among other things, they found that mineral deficiencies linked to high fructose corn syrup consumption make developing minds more susceptible to the neurotoxic effects of pesticides.

These various recent studies show how complex the path to our current autism epidemic has been. But evidence suggests that pesticide exposure—particularly during pregnancy—is implicated in a number of ways. . . .

Chemicals Contributing to Autism

In 2012 a group of researchers led by Philip Landrigan, M.D., of the Mount Sinai Medical Center, released a list of ten types of chemicals most likely to be linked to the development of autism. The group laid out an urgent strategy for research into the role of these contaminants and how children can be better protected from them. The list includes both commonly used organophosphate pesticides and long-lasting organochlorine pesticides, as well as other chemicals commonly found in consumer products.

Lead	Endocrine disruptors
Methylmercury	Automotive exhaust
Polychlorinated biphenyls	Polycyclic aromatic hydrocarbons
Organophosphate pesticides	Brominated flame retardants
Organochlorine pesticides	Perflourinated compounds

Taken from: Pesticide Action Network North America, 2012.

The Harm to IQ

Pesticide exposure during pregnancy can have dramatic effects on cognitive development. From a wide range of animal research to studies tracking the intellectual development of children over time, the evidence points squarely at prenatal pesticide exposures as significantly harming the development and functioning of the brain. These harms can then lead to both lower IQ levels and neurodevelopmental delays.

- A particularly compelling study used Magnetic Resonance Imaging (MRI) technology to observe the developing brains of infants who had been exposed to chlorpyrifos during pregnancy. Researchers observed significant structural changes, including abnormal areas of thinning and enlargement. Areas of the brain related to attention, language, reward systems, emotions and control were affected.
- Three cohort studies released in 2011 document cognitive impairment caused by exposure to organophosphates in the

womb. The first study found that higher metabolite levels in a mother's urine late in pregnancy increased the likelihood of reduced cognitive development in their children. The second study linked prenatal exposure to a seven-point reduction in IQ by age seven. The third study found that even very low levels of chlorpyrifos residues in cord blood resulted in lower IQ and reduced working memory.

- Pregnant mothers exposed to chlorpyrifos through household use (before this use was withdrawn) had infants with lower birth weight and reduced head circumference, both indicators of impaired cognitive ability later in childhood.
- Exposure to the organophosphate pesticides diazinon and parathion during early childhood may reduce cognitive function, according to results from animal studies. Low-dose exposures caused changes in the developing brains of rats known to correspond to reduced ability to learn. Other animal studies indicate that *in utero* and neonatal exposure to organophosphates increases the risk of developmental delays.
- Children at three months of age who were most highly exposed to the pyrethroid pesticide synergist piperonyl butoxide, as assessed by personal air monitors, scored 3.9 points lower on the Bayley Mental Developmental Index. These scores are predictive of school readiness, and the authors described their results as modest, yet "worrisome."
- Prenatal exposure to the DDT breakdown product DDE is also associated with neurodevelopmental delays in children, especially the "psychomotor" skills linking movement or muscular activity with mental processes. And exposure *in utero* to DDT itself has been associated with reduced cognitive functioning, memory and verbal skills among preschoolers.

Strong emerging evidence links childhood pesticide exposure to other, adult-onset neurological effects such as Parkinson's and Alzheimer's diseases; these studies are not examined here.

Our Children Pay the Price

The combined, society-wide impact of the various syndromes, disorders and deficits resulting from damage to children's brains and nervous systems early in life is immense. Health professionals and educators across the country have indicated concern that our current policies don't adequately protect our children as their nervous systems develop. Something must be done to address this gap, as the results of such exposures have profound consequences for individuals, families and society as a whole.

EVALUATING THE AUTHOR'S ARGUMENTS:

To make its argument that reducing pesticide exposure can reduce autism, PANNA cites numerous reports and studies. Which study did you find most compelling and relevant to the group's argument? Why?

Evidence of a Link Between Pesticide Exposure and Autism Is Rare

Emily Willingham

"Very little published evidence suggests a link between autism diagnoses and pesticide exposures."

In the following viewpoint Emily Willingham argues that autism is likely unrelated to pesticide exposure. She criticizes a report by Pesticide Action Network North America (PANNA) that claims that a sizable portion of all autism cases can be attributed either to direct pesticide exposure or to the way in which pesticides interact with people's genetic predispositions. Yet Willingham says PANNA bases its claims on reports and studies that found no such thing. She examines the studies and reports PANNA used and concludes that most of the original studies do not make these conclusions about autism or do not address autism specifically. Willingham accuses PANNA of exaggerating the amount of research on the autism-pesticide link and misleading readers into thinking studies have found a link when most have not. Willingham says the pesticide-autism link is not compelling, and groups like PANNA behave unethically when they misrepresent the available science on the topic. Willingham is a former biology professor. She writes frequently on autism and other science topics in *Scientific American*, *Slate*, and *Forbes*, where this viewpoint was originally published.

AS YOU READ, CONSIDER THE FOLLOWING QUESTIONS:
1. What problem does Willingham have with the fact that autism was mentioned fifty-eight times in a forty-page report about pesticides?
2. What problem does Willingham have with PANNA's use of a 2006 report that the group says proves a link between pesticides and autism?
3. What problem does Willingham have with PANNA's use of three studies from 2012 that the group says prove a link between pesticides and autism?

An anti-pesticide manifesto from the Pesticide Action Network North America (PANNA) has recently made a few headlines in big papers and nabbed a feature on an NPR [National Public Radio] member station with claims that "children today are sicker than they were a generation ago" and that pesticides are a "key driver" of the increase in childhood disorders such as "childhood cancers . . . autism, birth defects, and asthma." The news reports almost invariably describe the tome in scientific terms without mentioning that it's self published and not peer reviewed and contains no new data or information. The stories do not fail, however, to mention autism and to mention it early.

Stories That Sell

The PANNA authors pin their autism claim in part on the much written-about "autism epidemic." While environmental factors might play some role in a small portion of the increase in autism, . . . the general consensus appears to be that diagnostic substitution and enhanced awareness and recognition are the main drivers. Regardless of whether a genuine increase exists and what environmental factors are key to it, very little published evidence suggests a link between autism diagnoses and pesticide exposures. Yet the two keep popping up together in articles that sensationalize a relationship or posit one from research that doesn't address autism at all.

Autism, though, sells. It sells stories, it gets attention, it attracts clicks. So let's take a look at what they're selling you.

Claiming a Link by Misappropriating Research

The PANNA report mentions autism 58 times but focuses on it only in one short section of its 40 pages. In this section, called "The Science," the authors cite a handful of published reports, not all of them studies. One paper is a scientific op-ed of sorts that gained fame for asserting that "10 chemicals"—gotta love numbered lists—need attention in the context of autism, which sounds great except . . . hardly any of them had been linked to autism in any way. Against the backdrop of this editorial, the authors of the PANNA report then go on to list eight other studies they claim support an autism-pesticide

The author accuses Pesticide Action Network North America of exaggerating the amount of research on the autism-pesticide link and misleading readers into thinking studies have found a link when most have not.

link (I note here that the term "pesticide" is used loosely to encompass herbicides, fungicides, and insecticides). In four of eight cases, they simply mischaracterize the studies they cite.

Among the eight studies, an original research study they reference is a 2006 report assessing links between a pesticide, chlorpyrifos, and developmental delays (not diagnosed autism) in urban-dwelling families. Chlorpyrifos was introduced in 1965 and widely used in households until it was banned in 2001 for home use. It remains in wide use in agriculture. A second study the PANNA authors cite was a 2007 article describing prenatal agricultural exposure to several compounds, including chlorpyrifos. Those investigators found no link between chlorpyrifos and endpoints that were similar to those of [the] 2006 study, but did identify an association between another chemical and pervasive developmental disorders (again, not diagnosed autism). So far, we've got two reports with conflicting results that don't involve diagnosed autism.

The Arguments Fall Apart

The PANNA group then lists what they call a "trio of US studies" from 2012 that "examined links between environmental exposures among parents (including but not limited to pesticides) and the incidence of autism among their children." The studies in question didn't examine those links at all and don't mention pesticides or even environment; the authors of those reports might be surprised to see how their work has been described. All three are genetics studies. One group described finding a greater rate of spontaneous mutations passed along from fathers compared to mothers and that accumulation of these mutations was associated with the dad's age. Another found an association between an epilepsy-related gene variant and autism. The third iden-

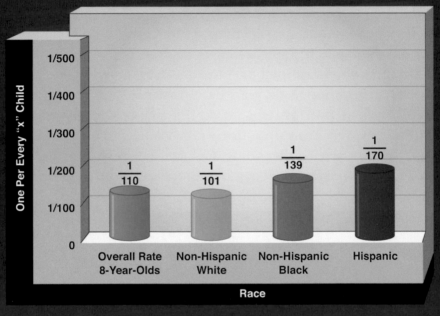

Autism rates vary by race and ethnicity. Some argue this casts doubt on theories that pesticide or other chemical exposure could be to blame, and suggests there is a genetic component to the disorder.

Taken from: National Institute of Mental Health and the Centers for Disease Control and Prevention's Autism and Developmental Disabilities Monitoring Network, 2006.

tified two other gene variants that are risk factors for autism. These studies weren't about pesticides and autism and they did not "examine links" in the way described. A fourth study the PANNA authors cite, also from 2012, was another genetics study that confirmed an association between father's age and accumulated mutations and was not a study of pesticides.

Finally, the PANNA report cites, as its last pillar in its "pesticides as key drivers of autism" argument, a 2012 paper proposing a hazy network between autism and a mishmash of high-fructose corn syrup consumption, mercury, organophosphates, and a host of other chemophobia bugbears. But that paper was a review and contained no new data. At the time of its publication, I analyzed its rationales and conclusions and found that the arguments fell apart from the word go. . . .

The Pesticide-Autism Link Is Not Compelling

In sum, the section from this PANNA report asserting that pesticides are a "key driver" of an autism increase contains eight citations of what they call "The Science." Two contain no original research, four aren't related to pesticide assessment at all but are misleadingly described as such, and two address intense pesticide exposure and pervasive developmental disorders and delays but not autism specifically. The case they build to link autism and pesticides is not a compelling one. Why did they build it? I'm guessing because autism gets attention. . . .

Current studies—animal or human—showing a link are vanishingly rare, even though six years have passed since the chlorpyrifos/urban families report first appeared. This lack of data again leads to the question: Why bring up autism in the PANNA report at all, much less 58 times, asserting that pesticides are a "key driver" of the condition? And why misrepresent half of the studies cited that pertain to it?

EVALUATING THE AUTHOR'S ARGUMENTS:

In the previous viewpoint you were asked to identify which study you found most compelling and relevant to PANNA's argument about autism and pesticides. Now that you have read Emily Willingham's critique of the PANNA report, look at what she says about the specific study or report you selected. What is her criticism of it? Does her assessment change your opinion of whether the study is compelling and relevant? Why or why not?

Viewpoint

5

Cures for Autism May Hurt Children More than Help Them

"Children with autism should not be subjected to testing and treatment that is not supported by good evidence of efficacy and safety— especially if it lacks any scientific rationale."

Michael Fitzpatrick

Society must end its frantic search for miracle cures to autism, argues Michael Fitzpatrick in the following viewpoint. He explains that families are understandably desperate to cure their children's autism—but he is disturbed that they seem willing to try nonscientific, and even harmful, miracle cures and treatments that border on quackery, in his opinion. He explains that autistic children are harmed when their parents drag them from appointment to appointment, subjecting them to invasive testing, painful procedures (like gastroscopies and colonoscopies), and other treatments that have no basis in science. In Fitzpatrick's opinion, a child's worth and humanity is lost in the frantic search for miracle cures. He urges society to try to accept autism; if cures must be sought, they should be based only on sound science and put a child's best interests first. Fitzpatrick is a doctor and author of the book *Defending Autism: A Damaging Delusion.*

Michael Fitzpatrick, "It's Time to Stop This 'Miracle Cure' Madness," Spiked.com, March 23, 2009. Reproduced with permission.

AS YOU READ, CONSIDER THE FOLLOWING QUESTIONS:
  1. Who is Nina Ltief and how does she factor into the author's argument?
  2. Who is Dr. T. Michael Culp and how does he factor into the author's argument?
  3. How much does Fitzpatrick estimate families with autistic children spend on biomedical tests and treatment each year?

Under the headline 'Can you ever cure autism? This mother believes her sons have recovered', the UK [United Kingdom] *Daily Mirror* recently told the story of Nina Ltief and her autistic twins, Eli and Christian, aged 7. According to the report, two years ago [in 2007] Nina was finding life with her sons so difficult that she was considering 'putting them into residential care'. But after discovering the 'unorthodox biomedical' approach, which includes a wide range of treatments, including special diets, vitamins and supplements, detoxification and medication with antibiotics, antifungals, antivirals and other drugs, her family life was dramatically transformed.

"Miracles" Are Not Science

The impact of the treatments was rapid, indeed 'miraculous':

- 'Within a few days of giving them enzymes which help digest wheat and dairy, they were sleeping better and, miraculously, began speaking';
- 'Two weeks later', after giving them a special vitamin supplement 'to help with gastrointestinal problems and support the immune system', their 'behaviour began improving and they started to do what they were told' (parents of children who are not autistic may wish to try this);
- After further tests, apparently revealing parasitic infestation and bowel inflammation, wheat and dairy products were excluded from the twins' diet: their speech and reading improved;
- A 'private psychologist' pronounced that, after 18 months on the biomedical programme, the twins were 'no longer on the autistic spectrum'.

Though it is well recognised that the behaviour of children with autism may improve over time, there is no plausible scientific mechanism through which these diverse treatments could achieve such dramatic results within such a short period. There is no scientific evidence that any of the specific treatments used can 'cure autism' or even improve the conduct or performance of children with autism. Furthermore, there is scant evidence for the safety of most of these interventions.

Many Autism Gurus Practice "High-Tech Hokum"

By her own account, Nina Ltief first discovered 'biomed' treatments at the first conference of the British parents' group Treating Autism in 2007. The group's second conference—promoted by the *Daily Mirror* report—took place last month [February 2009] in Bournemouth. I would like to be able to report in more detail on this conference, but after I asked a few questions at the first conference, I was banned from the recent event (even though I offered to attend to debate with any of the platform speakers). The guest of honour at both conferences was Dr Andrew Wakefield, the leading promoter of the (scientifically discredited) claim of a link between the MMR [measles, mumps, and rubella] vaccine and autism, now based in a private biomedical treatment clinic for autistic children in Texas. The Bournemouth course featured several prominent figures from the Defeat Autism Now! [DAN!] campaign in the USA, which links parents to DAN! practitioners (certified by attending a course lasting a few hours) and to a multi-million dollar network of laboratories and suppliers of dietary supplements, vitamins and other medications.

Let's look more closely at one of the Bournemouth platform speakers based in the UK: Dr T Michael Culp. The conference publicity explained that Dr Culp had acquired a 'medical degree' from Bastyr University, Seattle, and had subsequently worked as a 'family practice GP'. He had then become 'director of medical education' at a commercial lab, where he had developed 'innovative functional laboratory tests', before relocating to London. The organisers described Dr Culp as 'a world authority on Single Nucleotide Polymorphisms [SNPs], pronounced "snips"', helpfully explaining that SNPs 'can have a major impact on how we respond to things, such as viruses, toxins, bacteria and other assaults'. Dr Culp 'will explain how to test for SNPs believed to play a role in autism and how this information can be used to make treatment decisions'.

Close inspection of Dr Culp's qualifications reveals that these are MA.ND [master of arts and doctor of naturopathic medicine]: he is a doctor of naturopathy rather than conventional medicine (MD in the USA). Bastyr is a private college of naturopathy, not a conventional medical school. Though the title 'Dr' is widely used in the USA by osteopaths and dentists, as well as naturopaths and chiropracters, this is not common practice in Britain. Dr Culp's work as a 'family practice GP [general practitioner]' is not the sort of activity some of the parents attending the Treating Autism conference would understand as 'general practice': according to Dr Culp's website, he 'specialises in medical nutrition, botanical medicine, homeopathy, craniosacral therapy and several forms of mind-body healing'. Dr Culp claims experience in treating 'long-term illnesses', including chronic fatigue, depression, irritable bowel syndrome; he does not list any experience in relation to children with developmental disorders. His global status in research in genomics appears to have been achieved without having a single publication listed in the PubMed database. More than a decade ago he published an article entitled 'Vitamins and HIV therapy: a naturopathic perspective'.

Dr Culp runs a firm called Integrative Health Solutions Ltd, based in the Harley Street district in London, which offers a range of laboratory tests. One of the most popular is 'high resolution blood microscopy', a variation on the technique known as 'live blood analysis', now on offer in other autism treatment clinics. This test, involving

Fast Fact

In 2009 Denise Vowell, special master of the US Court of Federal Claims, noted in a court decision that an autistic boy had undergone 160 office visits, numerous lab tests that were not approved by the Food and Drug Administration, lumbar punctures, gut biopsies, and colonoscopies. She suggested that the invasive, painful procedures were unnecessary and unhelpful to his condition.

the projection of a blood film from a finger prick on to a screen for visual analysis, was dismissed more than 20 years ago by an American professor as 'high-tech hokum'. It has been promoted in the alternative health sector for the past 50 years as a method for the early detection of cancer, degenerative diseases and immune system dysfunctions. According to Edzard Ernst, professor of complementary medicine at the Peninsula Medical School, 'no credible scientific studies have demonstrated the reliability of "live blood analysis" for detecting any of the above conditions'. The same could be said for the value of tests for SNPs in guiding 'treatment decisions' in children with autism.

Fad Cures Are More Prevalent than Ever

Professionals experienced in the world of autism may object that there is nothing new about charismatic therapists offering miracle cures to parents. It is true that there is a long history of such interventions, including holding therapy and facilitated communication in the 1980s, secretin in the 1990s, and the more recent promotion of healing by dolphins, dogs or horses. It is also true that most parents are highly sceptical of the claims made by those who promote wonder cures.

But the current vogue for 'unorthodox biomedical' interventions has—with the help of the internet—developed more rapidly and had a wider impact than any of the earlier fads. Though the collapse of the litigation against MMR had a dampening effect on this movement in the UK (whereas in the USA a more resilient anti-vaccine campaign has boosted the biomedical network), it has gathered momentum over the past couple of years. New clinics have been established in Edinburgh, west London and south London. The pressures of the recession on the private medical sector appear to be encouraging clinics and practitioners who have previously treated adults complaining of chronic fatigue, allergies and other 'medically-unexplained' conditions, to diversify and seek to meet new 'needs'. Parents of children with autism, now commonly depicted as an epidemic condition, have become a focus for certain sections of the private medical sector. The investigations and treatments offered to children with autism are the same as those recommended for adults with diverse medical conditions: none is specific to autism.

Damage to Children and Family Budgets

Biomedical tests and treatments impose a heavy burden on families. One recent US estimate was of an average annual cost equivalent to the median household income ($50,000). Clearly such costs are far beyond the budgets of most British families who do not have private medical insurance (which may well not cover such costs). Yet, as a General Practitioner, I have come across families living on benefits who have spent a substantial proportion of their income on such interventions in the (forlorn) hope that this would help their autistic children. The opportunity costs—in terms of other expenditures of family resources that are sacrificed to biomedical interventions—may also be high, affecting siblings and the wider family.

It is important not to exaggerate the risks of biomedical interventions. They are mostly harmless as well as useless. However, this is not true of some of the more intensive treatments, such as heavy metal chelation therapy and the use of drugs such as anti-inflammatories and anti-virals. Testing, too, is not without its difficulties. The recent US vaccine court cases revealed children being subjected not only to repeated blood tests, but also to multiple gastroscopies, colonoscopies and lumbar punctures. The distress caused to autistic children and their families simply as a result of being dragged along to numerous clinic appointments should also not be underestimated.

However, the most damaging aspect of the crusade to 'cure autism' is not the treatments, but the attitude it expresses towards children with autism, indeed towards people with autism more broadly. Parents who share the unorthodox biomedical outlook project a negative view of autism, as a destructive disease process, drawing parallels with cancer or AIDS. They portray their children as being ill, listing their physical symptoms in the most graphic terms to illustrate the extent of their disease and disability. This rhetorical excess implicitly disparages and dehumanises people with autism. It is not surprising that such a negative outlook towards autism sometimes seems to lead to a negative attitude towards the autistic child, who is depicted in metaphors of toxicity and disease.

We Must Reject Pseudoscience and Quackery

What can we do to deter the damaging influence of the unorthodox biomedical approach? There is work here for both professionals and parents.

British doctor Andrew Wakefield (pictured) has been discredited for his views that autism is caused by the measles, mumps, and rubella vaccine.

For professionals, it must be a priority to uphold serious science against junk science and to establish a clear boundary between professional practice with a sound basis in medical science and practice lacking such a foundation. One of the tragedies of the MMR scandal is that it has taken more than 10 years for the full extent of the scientific critique of the Wakefield thesis to be articulated in the public realm. As a result, parents of autistic children—who were most harmed by this bad science—were the last to learn the truth. We need authoritative and rapid responses to claims that may appear scientific but lack adequate validation, and may foster false hopes among parents.

It is also important that mainstream scientists and doctors do not give legitimacy to pseudoscience and quackery. For example, the recent Treating Autism conference proudly proclaims the endorsement, 'The Royal College of Physicians has awarded the conference 10 credits for the two-day duration', presumably in recognition of its value for post-graduate education. The organisers were so pleased with this 'support' that it features, in bold print, in the model letter they recommend that delegates send to their GP accompanying a book on biomedical treatments. Mainstream specialists sometimes agree to appear as speakers at biomedical conferences, giving them the appearance of professional respectability (unfortunately, they do not appear in order to debate some of the biomedical lobby's claims, as I offered to do). Alternatively, organisers of mainstream conferences may invite representatives of the biomedical approach to speak at their conferences, despite their lack of relevant scientific or clinical expertise. The losers from this misguided collusion are parents for whom the distinctions between science and pseudoscience are blurred.

End the Miracle Cure Madness

For parents the priority must be to put the interests of the child first. Children with autism should not be subjected to testing and treatment that is not supported by good evidence of efficacy and safety—especially if it lacks any scientific rationale. Parents should be more critical of the claims made for biomedical interventions and more questioning of the qualifications, experience and expertise of those offering them. Parents' organisations should be wary of promoting the commercial interests of alternative practitioners and their associated laboratories and corporate suppliers of diets, pills and potions.

What our children need is less grieving and more accepting and loving as another human being—not just by their families but by others, too. We need an end to the miracle cure madness, and to give good steady science a chance to make long-term gains. For the present, we need to work on avoiding unnecessary despair and on developing a better understanding of what it means to be a valued human being.

EVALUATING THE AUTHOR'S ARGUMENTS:

Viewpoint author Michael Fitzpatrick criticizes many touted autism treatments as being based on flawed science or medical quackery and says a child's value, safety, and humanity are lost in the obsession to cure autism. If you were the parent of an autistic child, what lengths, if any, would you go to in order to cure or relieve his or her symptoms? Make a list of treatments you would attempt and treatments you would disregard, and the reasons why.

Viewpoint 6

Trying to Cure Autism Obscures People's Talents and Gifts

Tom Fields-Meyer

In the following viewpoint Tom Fields-Meyer argues that trying to eradicate autism denies the joy, skill, and talent autistic people bring to their families and communities. He discusses his teenage son Ezra, who was diagnosed with autism at two years old. Fields-Meyer explains that Ezra has a childlike enthusiasm for juvenile topics and also possesses a remarkable memory. Though some view these classically autistic traits as part of a lamentable disorder, he cannot imagine his son without them. He says autism is not a disease like cancer, which needs to be cured lest it claim ever more lives. Fields-Meyers thinks autism hinders certain abilities and skills but also highlights and embellishes others and makes people unique and wonderful. He would not want to live in a world that

"We can't separate Ezra from his disorder. Nor would we want to."

did not have autistic people, and he thinks his son would not be Ezra without his autism. He wishes science the best in its search for treatments and cures, but more important to him is delighting in his son's talents, skills, and unique perspective on the world. Fields-Meyer is a writer, journalist, and author of the memoir *Following Ezra: What One Father Learned About Gumby, Otters, Autism, and Love from His Extraordinary Son*.

AS YOU READ, CONSIDER THE FOLLOWING QUESTIONS:
1. What is "The Question," according to Fields-Meyer, and how does it make him feel?
2. What topics does the author say his son Ezra repeatedly talks about?
3. List at least two examples of Ezra's remarkable memory.

As the father of a teenage son with autism, I have coped with many challenges: finding the right school for a boy who can't sit still and has trouble connecting with peers; managing medications to help tame his anxiety and other symptoms; learning to negotiate endless one-sided conversations about my son's two obsessions—animated movies and animals.

But those demands have never annoyed me in the way The Question does. Rarely does a week pass without someone asking me: "So what do you think? What causes autism?"

Autism Is Not a Disease to Be Cured

This summer [2011] has seen a plethora of headlines on the topic. July brought news of a study showing an unexpectedly high occurrence of autism among fraternal twins, a finding that could implicate both genetic and environmental factors. Then new research revealed that younger siblings of children with the disorder have a 20 times greater chance of developing autism than the general population. Last month's [August 2011] story was British researcher Simon Baron Cohen's "assortative mating" theory. It speculates that parents who share certain tendencies—such as expertise in math and science—may produce children with a higher risk for autism.

So what's the parent of a living, breathing autism specimen to do with the constant barrage of speculation? My standard reply: I'm grateful that scientists are focusing on autism. I'm going to concentrate on my kid.

That's the simple answer. But it's actually more complex. When you read about studies on, say, breast cancer or juvenile diabetes, the objective is clear: to eradicate these awful diseases and save lives.

Autism, on the other hand, occurs on a spectrum. At one end are individuals who can barely communicate, can't care for themselves and seem lost in a constant blur of involuntary movements. At the other end are people with quirky dispositions, rigid personal habits and a tendency to speak and think obsessively about one or two subjects such as train schedules or insects.

Would We Really Want a World Without Autistic People?

My son falls somewhere in the middle: Ezra is verbal, but, at 15, he still tends to talk about the same things over and over: otters, Pixar movies, dog breeds. He doesn't rock or flap his hands much anymore,

Autism hinders certain abilities and skills of a child but also highlights and embellishes others, which, the author argues, makes autistic people unique and wonderful.

but his sensory challenges make it difficult to stay in one place, so he paces in math class and during recess while other kids are chatting with friends.

Like many people with autism, he also possesses a remarkable memory. He knows the running times of hundreds of animated films, has mastered the details of several animal encyclopedias and can recall the exact date in 2003 he first heard a woodpecker. Learning a new acquaintance's birthday, Ezra will charm the person by instantaneously announcing which Disney movie premiered on that exact date.

More important, he has remarkable enthusiasm for life, greeting days that are significant to him—the first of the month,

for example, or the day of the "Cars 2" premiere—by running around the house before dawn shouting with infectious delight.

When I hear that, I wonder: Would we really want a world without such people? Or without biologists with underdeveloped social skills who can focus obsessively on a particular breed of newt? Or without certain brilliant software engineers who might not make great dinner party guests? (The ultimate irony is that the kind of person who has the obsessive focus to isolate the combination of factors that cause autism might just have a touch of it himself.)

Science Is Good, but People Are Better

I'm pleased that so much money and brainpower is going toward investigating autism. Thirteen years ago, when Ezra was 2 and first displaying signs of the disorder, research on it was rare and parents like us weren't typically advised to be alert to its symptoms.

Now, thanks to advocacy groups like Autism Speaks (which merged in 2007 with the Los Angeles–based Cure Autism Now), the science is impressive. Fifty academic and research institutions are collaborating on the Autism Genome Project, the largest-ever study to find genes associated with inherited risk for autism.

Another program is tracking more than 2,000 infant siblings of children with autism to help discern environmental factors that might play a part. Few scientifically proven treatments are available to treat autism's symptoms, but now millions of private and government dollars are helping researchers to focus on finding them.

The increased understanding and public awareness this research brings can only be good.

As for our family, we often deal with our circumstances with black humor. Sometimes when Ezra has the flu or is knocked out by a fever, his behavior is radically transformed. Normally in constant motion, he slows down, cuddling quietly under the covers like any other sick kid. My wife looks at him, then at me, and smiles. "Maybe when he wakes up, he'll be cured," she says, as if some sci-fi movie magic could remove our son's autism.

It's our joke because we can't separate Ezra from his disorder. Nor would we want to. Ezra without the Pixar fixation, without the mental catalog of animal kingdom trivia, would not be Ezra. What would life in our house be like without a 15-year-old who wakes up once a month elated just because he gets to turn a new page on the calendar?

I'll be happy to know when they figure out the science. But I'll still be focused on my kid.

EVALUATING THE AUTHOR'S ARGUMENTS:

Viewpoint author Tom Fields-Meyer's sentiment that he would not want to live in a world without people like his son Ezra is a unique perspective not typically presented in debates over autism. What do you think? Should society view autistic people as not disabled but as enabled in certain areas? How can thinking of autistic people as gifted inform both society's response to them and scientific research into treatments and cures? Quote from the texts you have read in your answer.

Facts About Autism

Editor's note: These facts can be used in reports to add credibility when making important points or claims.

Facts About the Prevalence of Autism

The May Institute in Massachusetts maintains that autism:

- is diagnosed in one in every eighty-eight children;
- is found in all races, ethnicities, and social groups;
- occurs five times more often in boys than in girls;
- is more common than pediatric cancer, diabetes, and AIDS combined;
- is considered a national public health crisis by the Centers for Disease Control and Prevention (CDC); and
- has no known cause or cure.

According to the CDC:

- About 1 percent of people in Asia, Europe, and North America are autistic.
- Studies of identical twins show that if one child has autism, the other also has it 36 to 95 percent of the time. In nonidentical twins, if one child has autism, then the other is affected up to 31 percent of the time.
- The parents of a child with autism have a 2 to 18 percent chance of having a second autistic child.

The CDC has identified signs to help experts diagnose autism. Autistic children might

- have delayed speech and language skills;
- not respond to their name by twelve months old;
- not look at objects when someone points at them;
- prefer not to be held or cuddled;
- avoid eye contact and want to be alone;

- have trouble expressing their needs;
- lose skills they once had or stop saying words they had previously learned;
- have trouble understanding people's emotions or talking about their own feelings;
- repeat words, phrases, or actions over and over;
- give unrelated answers to questions;
- have trouble adapting to minor changes;
- flap their hands, spin in circles, or rock back and forth;
- have unusual reactions to the way things sound, smell, taste, look, or feel;
- appear to be unaware when people talk to them; and
- be interested in people but not know how to talk, play with, or relate to them.

Facts About the Causes of Autism

A 2012 report by the Interagency Autism Coordinating Committee maintains that autism may be caused by genetic factors but also identified several environmental risks:

- Genetics:
    - In 2009 it was believed that genes, passed down from a mother and father to their child, may be the cause of up to 10 percent of autism cases. By 2012 genetics were found to be responsible in 25 percent of cases.
    - There are as many as one thousand rare changes or mutations in genes that may increase a person's risk of autism.
    - A blood test would not be able to show these changes in a mother's or father's genes and therefore would not be helpful in determining their risk of having a baby with autism.

- Environmental Risks:
    - Diet, prescription drugs, and toxic chemicals may be linked to autism.
    - Ten chemicals may be linked to the development of autism, including lead, mercury, insecticides, car exhaust, and flame retardants.

- Researchers found evidence that when women take vitamins in the months before and after they get pregnant, the risk of their baby being autistic declines.
- A 2012 analysis of studies showed that older mothers are more likely to have a child with autism.
- A 2011 analysis found that babies born to older fathers also have an increased risk of developing autism.

According to the American Academy of Pediatrics:

- Scientific studies have shown there is no link between autism and thimerosal, a mercury-based preservative used in some vaccines.
- A study in California showed that after thimerosal was removed from most childhood vaccines by 2002, cases of autism did not decline.
- The American Medical Association, the CDC, and the Institute of Medicine (IOM) all maintain there is no association between thimerosal in vaccines and autism.
- The National Institute of Child Health and Human Development asserts that there is no definite, scientific proof that any vaccine or combination of vaccines can cause autism. On the contrary, vaccines help the immune system defend the body.

Facts About Treatment of Autism

According to the Mayo Clinic, there is not yet a cure for autism, but treatment options include

- behavior and communication therapy to teach children how to act in social situations or how to communicate better;
- educational therapy with highly structured programs and activities designed to improve social skills, behavior, and communication;
- family therapies to teach parents and family members how to interact with children in ways that promote social interaction skills, manage problem behaviors, and improve daily living skills;
- medications, which cannot cure autism but may help control symptoms—antidepressants, antipsychotics, and other drugs—may be prescribed for children who are anxious or hyperactive, for example; and

• alternative and complementary therapies. Special diets are thought to help manage autism, but more research into their effectiveness is needed. Chelation therapy has been suggested to flush mercury and other heavy metals from the body. However, there is no proven link between mercury and autism, and chelation therapy can cause harm and even death.

Facts About the Costs of Autism

According to Autism Speaks:

• Autism costs Americans $126 billion per year.
• Costs associated with autism in the United States have more than tripled since 2006.
• The cost of lifetime care for an autistic American is $1.4 million.
• About 45 percent of autistic people also have intellectual disabilities. Their cost of lifetime care is about $2.3 million.

Opinions About Autism

According to a poll conducted for the National Alliance for Autism Research:

• Most Americans (71 percent) know that diagnosed cases of autism are increasing, not decreasing.
• Thirty-nine percent of respondents say they have no idea how many Americans have autism.
• One in five respondents (20 percent) report that they have a close friend or relative who has autism.
• Almost one-third, 30 percent, of Americans cannot identify even one warning sign of autism.
• One in four people think that most autistic children excel in math, and 39 percent believe that autistic children are generally smarter than average children. In reality, only a small percentage of people with autism display exceptional skills in math.
• Four out of five people know that the statement that there are only minor differences between autistic and retarded children is false.
• More than 70 percent of respondents say they are concerned about autism.

- Nearly one in five (19 percent) say that they have been concerned that their child or a relative's child may have autism, and 27 percent of parents are concerned that their child or grandchild might develop autism.
- Nearly seven in ten Americans (69 percent) worry that many cases of autism go undiagnosed because there is no reliable test for the condition.
- More than four in five Americans (85 percent) support legislation to increase funding for genetics research that seeks a cure for autism.

Organizations to Contact

The editors have compiled the following list of organizations concerned with the issues debated in this book. The descriptions are derived from materials provided by the organizations. All have publications or information available for interested readers. The list was compiled on the date of publication of the present volume; the information provided here may change. Be aware that many organizations take several weeks or longer to respond to inquiries, so allow as much time as possible for the receipt of requested materials.

Autism Program at Yale
Child Study Center, Yale School of Medicine
Yale University
230 S. Frontage Rd.
New Haven, CT 06519
(203) 785-2540
website: http://childstudycenter.yale.edu/autism/index.aspx

One of the leading research centers in the world, the Autism Program at Yale is an interdisciplinary group of clinicians and scholars dedicated to providing comprehensive clinical services to children with autism spectrum disorders and their families. The program involves infants, toddlers, preschoolers, school-age children, and young adults (aged eighteen to twenty-one) with autism and related disorders. It integrates highly experienced professionals from the fields of clinical psychology, neuropsychology and neuroimaging, child psychiatry, speech-language pathology, social work, genetics and the biological sciences, and psychopharmacology and psychiatric nursing. Descriptions of ongoing research are available on the website.

Autism Research Institute
4182 Adams Ave.
San Diego, CA 92116
website: www.autism.com

This organization, founded by Bernard Rimland, maintains that autism is treatable. The institute offers a support network for parents and diagnosed individuals, provides resources for adults who have an autism spectrum disorder, and sponsors research on the topic.

Autism Science Foundation

28 W. Thirty-Ninth St., Ste. 502
New York, NY 10018
(212) 391-3913
e-mail: contactus@autismsciencefoundation.org
website: www.autismsciencefoundation.org

The Autism Science Foundation's mission is to support autism research by providing funding and other assistance to scientists and organizations that conduct, facilitate, publicize, and disseminate autism research. The foundation operates from the belief that autism has a strong genetic component and that vaccines do not contribute to autism. In addition to publishing a newsletter and a blog, the foundation funds numerous research studies and posts a multitude of links to breaking news and research about autism on its website.

Autism Society

4340 East-West Hwy., Ste. 350
Bethesda, MD 20814
(800) 328-8476
website: www.autism-society.org

The Autism Society is the nation's leading grassroots autism organization. It aims to increase public awareness about the day-to-day issues faced by people on the spectrum, advocate for appropriate services for individuals across their life span, and provide the latest information regarding treatment, education, research, and advocacy. The Autism Society has spearheaded numerous pieces of state and local legislation, including the 2006 Combating Autism Act, the first federal autism-specific law. The society publishes the quarterly journal *Autism Advocate* and also a *Living with Autism* series.

Autism Speaks

One E. Thirty-Third St., 4th Fl.
New York, NY 10016

(888) 288-4762
e-mail: familyservices@autismspeaks.org
website: www.autismspeaks.org

This leading autism science and advocacy organization is dedicated to funding research into the causes, prevention, treatments, and cure for autism; increasing awareness of autism spectrum disorders; and advocating for the needs of individuals with autism and their families. The organization posts a wide variety of autism-related news, research, and other information. In addition to research, it sponsors Walk Now for Autism Speaks, a national walkathon that has raised millions of dollars for autism research.

Foundation for Autism Information & Research
1300 Jefferson Rd.
Hoffman Estates, IL 60169
e-mail: info@autismmedia.org
website: www.autismmedia.org

This nonprofit foundation creates original, up-to-date, and comprehensive educational media (in the form of video documentaries) to inform the medical community and the public about the latest advances in research and biomedical and behavioral therapies for autism spectrum disorders. Its current projects include an ever-expanding media center that features excerpts of video interviews of speakers who present at various national autism conferences. These and other sources of media can be viewed on the foundation's website.

Generation Rescue
13636 Ventura Blvd., #259
Sherman Oaks, CA 91423
(877) 98-288476
website: www.generationrescue.org

This organization is led by actress Jenny McCarthy, whose son Evan was diagnosed with autism in 2005. Generation Rescue offers information about vaccines, diets, and other findings related to possible causes and treatments of autism. It pairs parents of newly diagnosed children with mentors who can guide them through the often arduous process of getting services and information.

National Autism Association
20 Alice Agnew Dr.
Attleboro Falls, MA 02763
(877) 622-2884
website: http://nationalautismassociation.org

About twenty-five thousand parents belong to the National Autism Association, an advocacy organization and leading voice on issues related to severe autism, regressive autism, autism safety, autism abuse, and crisis prevention. The group's mission is to respond to the most urgent needs of the autism community, providing help and hope so that all affected can reach their full potential. The group publishes numerous papers and articles, including "Lethal Outcomes in Autism Spectrum Disorders—2012" and "Behind Closed Doors: What's Happening to Students with Autism in America's Public Schools?" These and other materials are available on the group's website.

Organization for Autism Research (OAR)
2000 N. Fourteenth St., Ste. 710
Arlington, VA 22201
(703) 243-9710
website: www.researchautism.org

OAR's mission is to apply research to the challenges of autism. OAR defines applied research as research that directly impacts the day-to-day quality of life of learners with autism. It entails the systematic investigation of variables associated with positive outcomes in such areas as education, communication, self care, social skills, employment, behavior, and adult and community living. OAR funds pilot studies and targeted research whose outcomes offer new insights into the behavioral and social development of individuals with autism with an emphasis on communication, education, and vocational challenges. Its publications include the *OARacle* newsletter and the *Life Journey Through Autism* series, which can be downloaded for free from its website.

SafeMinds
16033 Bolsa Chica St., #104-142
Huntington Beach, CA 92649
(404) 934-0777
website: www.safeminds.org

SafeMinds was founded to raise awareness, support research, change policy, and focus national attention on the link between mercury and neurological disorders such as autism, attention deficit disorder, language delay, and learning difficulties. The group's goal is to eliminate mercury from all medical products, including vaccines, and to substantially reduce other environmental exposures to mercury.

US Autism and Asperger Association
12180 S. 300 E. #532
Draper, UT 84020-0532
(888) 928-8476
website: www.usautism.org

The mission of this nonprofit organization is to provide the opportunity for everyone with autism spectrum disorders to achieve their fullest potential, by enriching the autism community with education, training, accessible resources, and partnerships with local and national projects. The association provides numerous resources for people living with autism and their family members, caregivers, medical professionals, teachers, and others. It publishes a weekly newsletter called *USAAA WeeklyNews* that is available on its website, along with numerous other materials and videos.

US Department of Health and Human Services
Interagency Autism Coordinating Committee (IACC)
200 Independence Ave. SW
Washington, DC 20201
e-mail: IACCPublicInquiries@mail.nih.gov
website: http://iacc.hhs.gov

The IACC was established in accordance with the Combating Autism Act of 2006 and was reauthorized by the Combating Autism Reauthorization Act of 2011. It is a federal advisory committee mandated by Congress to coordinate autism spectrum disorder–related activities across the US Department of Health and Human Services. Some of its numerous publications included *The 2012 IACC Strategic Plan Update*, which focuses on recent advances and emerging opportunities in autism research, and *The New Genetics of Autism—Why Environment Matters*.

For Further Reading

Books

Goldberg, Michael, and Elyse Goldberg. *The Myth of Autism: How a Misunderstood Epidemic Is Destroying Our Children.* New York: Skyhorse, 2011. The authors argue that autism is not genetic, but rather the symptom of a treatable neurological disease that attacks the brain's immune system.

Grandin, Temple. *Thinking in Pictures: My Life with Autism.* New York: Vintage, 2010. One of the best-known and most accomplished persons with autism, Temple Grandin is a scientist. In this book she documents how she managed to breach the boundaries of autism to function in the world around her.

Montgomery, Sy, and Temple Grandin. *How the Girl Who Loved Cows Embraced Autism and Changed the World.* New York: Houghton Mifflin, 2012. This book tells the story of Temple Grandin, a scientist and professor of animal science at Colorado State University.

Offit, Paul A. *Autism's False Prophets: Bad Science, Risky Medicine, and the Search for a Cure.* New York: Columbia University Press, 2010. A national expert on vaccines argues that vaccines are not to blame for autism. He suggests that facts have been dangerously manipulated in the search for the cause of autism, making people susceptible to bad science and risky behavior.

Olmsted, Dan, and Mark Blaxill. *The Age of Autism: Mercury, Medicine, and a Man-Made Epidemic.* New York: Thomas Dunne, 2010. Traces the long overlooked history of mercury poisoning and its connection to autism.

Periodicals

Bean, Shawn. "My Son Had Autism. Then He Didn't," *Huffington Post*, January 22, 2012. www.huffingtonpost.com/shawn-bean/my -son-had-autism-then-he_b_2498908.html.

Becker, Jody. "Behind the Autism Statistics," *Atlantic*, October 2009. www.theatlantic.com/magazine/archive/2009/10/behind-the -autism-statistics/307729.

Belluz, Julia. "The Battle over the 'Cure' for Autism," *Maclean's*, January 26, 2012. www2.macleans.ca/2012/01/26/the-battle-over-the-cure-for-autism.

Berrington, Lucy. "The Case Against Asperger's," *Asperger's Alive* (blog), *Psychology Today*, October 21, 2012. www.psychology today.com/blog/aspergers-alive/201210/the-case-against-aspergers.

Chung, Winston. "Rise in Autism Could Be Overestimated," *City Brights* (blog), *San Francisco Chronicle*, April 2, 2012. http://blog .sfgate.com/wchung/2012/04/02/rise-in-autism-could-be-over estimated.

Cook, Gareth. "The Autism Advantage," *New York Times*, December 2, 2012. www.nytimes.com/2012/12/02/magazine/the-autism -advantage.html.

Disabled World. "TV Implicated in Autism Rise in US," July 16, 2010. www.disabled-world.com/health/neurology/autism/tv-impli cated.php.

Dunkle, Margaret. "We Don't Know Enough About Childhood Vaccines," *Baltimore Sun*, July 11, 2011. http://articles.baltimore sun.com/2011-07-11/news/bs-ed-vaccines-illness-20110711_1 _doses-childhood-vaccines-mmr.

England, Breck. "Provide More Services for Autistic Kids," *Salt Lake City Deseret News*, April 13, 2012. www.deseretnews.com /article/765568214/Provide-more-services-for-autistic-kids .html?pg=all.

Fischkin, Barbara. "An Autism Mother Rages: Television DOES NOT Cause Autism," *Huffington Post*, February 27, 2007. www .huffingtonpost.com/barbara-fischkin/an-autism-mother-rages -te_b_42230.html.

Frances, Allen. "Psychiatric Fads and Overdiagnosis," *DSM5 in Distress* (blog), *Psychology Today*, June 2, 2010. www.psychologytoday.com /blog/dsm5-in-distress/201006/psychiatric-fads-and-overdiagnosis.

Geier, Mark. "My Therapy Is Unconventional, but It Works," *Baltimore Sun*, June 16, 2011. http://articles.baltimoresun.com /2011-06-16/news/bs-ed-autism-doctor-20110616_1_autism -doctor-hormone-levels-research-in-peer-reviewed-journals.

Gold, Claudia M. "In Autism, Medication Is Only a Partial Answer," *Boston Globe*, December 14, 2009. www.boston.com/bostonglobe /editorial_opinion/oped/articles/2009/12/14/in_autism_medica tion_is_only_a_partial_answer.

Grant, Bob. "Opening a Can of Worms," *Scientist*, February 1, 2011. www.the-scientist.com/?articles.view/articleNo/30802/title /Opening-a-Can-of-Worms.

Gray, Josyln. "Asperger's Is Over-Diagnosed? You Try Getting Your Kid Evaluated," *Babble*, February 1, 2012. www.babble.com/mom /aspergers-is-over-diagnosed-try-getting-your-kid-evaluated.

Greenfield, Karl Taro. "Growing Old with Autism," *New York Times*, May 23, 2009. www.nytimes.com/2009/05/24/opinion /24greenfeld.html?pagewanted=all.

Jones, Lon. "What We Are Not Looking at with Autism," OpEdNews .com, October 2, 2012. www.opednews.com/articles/What-we-are -not-looking-at-by-Lon-Jones-121002-205.html.

Kristof, Nicholas D. "Do Toxins Cause Autism?," *New York Times*, Februrary 24, 2010. www.nytimes.com/2010/02/25/opinion /25kristof.html?_r=0.

Los Angeles Times. "An Autism Bill Worth Funding," September 30, 2011. http://articles.latimes.com/2011/sep/30/opinion/la-ed -autism-20110930.

Marcotte, Amanda. "More Caution on Autism Op-Eds, Please," *XX Factor* (blog), *Slate*, February 26, 2010. www.slate.com/blogs /xx_factor/2010/02/26/using_alarmist_language_about_autism _doesnt_help_an_already_ugly_situation.html.

McCarthy, Jenny. "My Son's Recovery from Autism," CNN, April 4, 2008. www.cnn.com/2008/US/04/02/mccarthy.autsimtreatment /index.html.

McDowall, Melanie. "Men's 'Biological Clock' Linked to Schizophrenia and Autism," *Conversation*, October 23, 2012. http://theconversation.edu.au/mens-biological-clock-linked-to -schizophrenia-and-autism-9877.

Moench, Brian. "Utah's Alarming Autism Rate," *Salt Lake Tribune*, April 7, 2012. www.sltrib.com/sltrib/opinion/53862628-82 /autism-utah-autistic-environmental.html.csp.

Nugent, Benjamin. "I Had Asperger Syndrome. Briefly," *New York Times*, December 1, 2012. www.nytimes.com/2012/02/01 /opinion/i-had-asperger-syndrome-briefly.html.

Paregol, Ian. "Maryland Again Fails Autism Community," *Baltimore Sun*, April 19, 2012. www.baltimoresun.com/news/opinion/oped /bs-ed-autism-20120419,0,4484079.story.

Richards, Sabrina. "Can Worms Alleviate Autism?," *Scientist*, November 27, 2012. www.the-scientist.com/?articles.view/article No/33463/title/Can-Worms-Alleviate-Autism-.

Senator, Susan. "My Autistic Son's Step into the Wider World—Through Facebook," *Washington Post*, August 10, 2012. http:// articles.washingtonpost.com/2012-08-10/opinions/35493782_1 _nat-facebook-page-autistic-son.

Senator, Susan. "Tiger Mother to an Autistic Son," *Washington Post*, December 23, 2011. http://articles.washingtonpost.com/2011-12 -23/opinions/35284865_1_nat-autistic-son-school-professionals.

Shute, Nancy. "Desperation Drives Parents to Dubious Autism Treatments," *Scientific American*, October 7, 2010. www.scientific american.com/article.cfm?id=desperate-for-an-autism-cure.

Steinberg, Paul. "Asperger's History of Overdiagnosis," *New York Times*, January 31, 2012. www.nytimes.com/2012/02/01/opinion /aspergers-historv-of-over-diagnosis.html.

Sullum, Jacob. "If You Recover from Asperger's, You Never Really Had It," *Hit & Run* (blog), *Reason*, February 1, 2012. http://reason .com/blog/2012/02/01/if-you-recover-from-aspergers-you-never.

Waldman, Katy. "Do Child Prodigies Owe Their Talents to Autism?," *Browbeat* (blog), *Slate*, July 10, 2012. www.slate.com/blogs/brow beat/2012/07/10/child_prodigies_autistic_new_study_suggests_a _link_between_autism_and_child_prodigies_.html.

Wallace, James P. "A Big Brother's View of Autism," *Newsday*, December 2, 2011. www.newsday.com/opinion/oped/expressway -a-big-brother-s-view-of-autism-1.3363044.

Wang, Shirley S. "Who Can Outgrow or Recover from Autism," *Wall Street Journal*, January 22, 2012. http://online.wsj.com/article/SB1 0001424127887323301104578255721887372386.html.

Willingham, Emily. "No Evidence Supporting Chelation as Autism Treatment," *Forbes*, November 30, 2012. www.forbes.com/sites /emilywillingham/2012/11/30/no-evidence-supporting-chelation -as-autism-treatment.

Xu, Jennifer. "Autism as an Identity, Not a Disease," *Michigan Daily* (University of Michigan, Ann Arbor), September 27, 2012. www.michigandaily.com/arts/melanie-yergeau-autistic-self -advocacy?page=0,0.

Yudell, Michael. "And the Latest Cause of Autism Is . . .," *The Public's Health* (blog), *Philadelphia Inquirer*, September 5, 2012. www .philly.com/philly/blogs/public_health/And-the-latest-cause-of -autism-is———-.html.

Zarembo, Alan. "Autism Boom: An Epidemic of Disease or Discovery?," *Los Angeles Times*, December 11, 2011. www.latimes .com/news/local/autism/la-me-autism-day-one-html,0,1218038 .htmlstory.

Websites

Age of Autism (www.ageofautism.com). This publication, which calls itself the "Daily Web Newspaper of the Autism Epidemic," has published hundreds of articles, blog entries, and other posts since its launch in November 2007. Most of the materials are from the perspective that autism is an environmentally induced illness that is treatable.

American Psychiatric Association DSM-5 Development (www .dsm5.org/Pages/Default.aspx). This is the website of the fifth edition of the *Diagnostic and Statistical Manual of Mental Disorders* (DSM-5), which was published in May 2013. The DSM-5 contains a controversial revision to what qualifies as an autism spectrum disorder. The DSM-5 website contains press releases related to the changes and other information regarding how the new edition was conceived.

Autism Action Network (http://autismactionnetwork.org). This national, nonpartisan political action organization was formed by parents in support of children with neurodevelopmental and communication disorders. The network seeks to advance public policy on autism-related issues and support political candidates who share its goals in state and federal elections. The website features the latest stories of autism in the news, such as political developments regarding autism, and helps visitors contact their elected representatives on autism-related matters.

Autism File (www.autismfile.com). This bimonthly magazine deals with all aspects of autism, including vaccines, diet, nutrition, organizations, studies, new research, and other topics. Articles are written by parents, doctors, consultants, teachers, and other people related to the field of autism. The website contains information about articles included in each publication and general information about autism.

Global Autism Project (http://globalautismproject.org). This group partners with local autism centers to increase the global availability and efficacy of autism services. The website contains information on the group's activities and how various individuals and organizations can get involved.

Temple Grandin's Official Autism Website (www.templegrandin .com). This is the website of Temple Grandin, one of the most well-known and successful people with autism. Diagnosed when she was three years old, Grandin has become a prominent speaker and writer on the issue. Her website offers information on her activities and accomplishments.

Index

trying to cure, obscures
people's talents/gifts, 110–
114
vaccines are not associated
with risk of, 29–32
vaccines might be cause of,
21–28
See also Diagnosis; Symptoms;
Treatment(s)
Autism Insurance Act (NJ), 59
Autism Science Foundation,
83
Autism Speaks, 77
Autistic Self Advocacy Network,
58
Autoimmunity, 14–15

B
Baron-Cohen, Simon, 39, 40,
41, 42
Behavior therapy. *See* Applied
behavioral analysis
Beyerstein, Lindsay, 17
Blaxill, Mark, 24, 63
Brain
abnormal immune responses
in, 14
connections between immune
system and, 75–76
de novo mutations and
functioning of, 36
development, abnormal
cytokine production
during, 12
impacts of pesticide exposures
on, 87, 92–93
"male," assortative mating
theory and, 39–40
Brown, Ari, 81

C
Carpenter, Howard, 8
Casein, 77, 80
Centers for Disease Control and
Prevention (CDC), 29
on prevalence of autism, 7,
62, 67, 89–90
Chelation therapy, 8, 107
Child prodigies, prevalence of
autism among, 113
Children
changes in vaccines for, 30–31
increase in rates of autism in,
7, 45, 67, 89–90
numbers on federal disability
for autism, 69
Childs, Dan, 79
Chlorpyrifos, 92, 93, 98
Clinton administration, 67
Coury, Daniel, 81–82
Culp, T. Michael, 103–104
Cytokines, 8, 12–14

D
Daily Mirror (newspaper), 102,
103
DDT, 93
Developmental disabilities,
prevalence of, 88
Diagnosis
criteria for, 12, 53, 57–58
frequency of, 46–47
increase in, 39, *48*
*Diagnostic and Statistical Manual
of Mental Disorders* (DSM),
51–52, 57–58, *59*
Diet. *See* Gluten-/casein-free
diet
Down syndrome, 34

Picture Credits

© AP Images/PRNewsfoto, 63

© AP Images/Angelika Warmuth/picture-alliance/dpa, 54

© Art Directors & TRIP/Alamy, 89

© Bubbles Photolibrary/Alamy, 25

© Peter Cavanagh/Alamy, 36

© Kris Connor/Getty Images, 70

© Paul Doyle/Alamy, 112

© Gale, Cengage, 15, 26, 35, 48, 52, 64, 69, 76, 82, 92, 99, 105

© incamerastock/Alamy, 43

© Vicky Kasala/Alamy, 10

© David Lawrence/Alamy, 72

© Peter McDiarmid/Getty Images, 107

© Larry Muleville/Science Source, 13

© Photofusion Picture Library/Alamy, 84

© Nancy J. Pierce/Science Source, 46

© Robert Harding Picture Library/Alamy, 97

© Stockbroker/Alamy, 31

© Studio 101/Alamy, 59

© WILDLIFE GmbH/Alamy, 75